Elaine Walker
Steve Elsworth

New Edition

Grammar Practice

for Intermediate Students

with key

Longman

Pearson Education Limited
Edinburgh Gate, Harlow
Essex,
CM20 2JE, England.
And Associated Companies throughout the World.

www.longman-elt.com

© Pearson Education Limited 1986, 2000

ISBN 0 582 41716 3
Second impression 2001
Set in Slimbach

Printed in Spain by Mateu Cromo

Illustrations by David Mostyn

Project Managed by Lewis Lansford

Additional material written by David Bowker

Contents

To the Student

NOUNS AND ADJECTIVES

the article *a* and *the* 1–4
possessives 4–6
plurals 6–7
comparative and superlative adjectives 8–10
so and *such* 10

VERBS

The present tense
present simple and continuous 11–14

The past tense
past simple and continuous 15–16
present perfect 17–19
past perfect 20–22

The future tense
present continuous as future 25–26
going to future 25–26
future simple 25–26
present simple as future 27
future continuous 28–29
future perfect 30–31
future in the past 33

Simple, continuous, and perfect aspects 34–36

Verb formations
irregular verbs 37
verbs with gerund, infinitive, or indirect speech 38–42

The passive
passives 43–47
have something done 47–48

Miscellaneous
wish 48–53

CONDITIONALS

first conditional 54–55
second conditional 54–55
zero conditional 54–55
third conditional 56–57
words other than *if* 58
hidden conditionals 59
mixed tense conditionals 60

MODALS

modals in questions and negatives 63
can, could, be able to 64
must, have to 65–69
should, ought to 67–69
need 69–72
modals in past tense 73–76
could, would, might 76–77

GERUNDS AND INFINITIVES

The gerund 78–79
The infinitive 78, 80–84
gerund or infinitive 84–86

REPORTED SPEECH

Indirect speech 87–103

SENTENCE STRUCTURE

Word order
position of direct and indirect objects 104
order of adverbs 105–106
frequency adverbs 107–109
order of adjectives 109–110
link words 110–111

Questions and answers
who questions 111–112
tag questions 113–115
short answers 115–116
embedded questions and answers 116–119

Relative clauses 119–127

PREPOSITIONS AND PHRASAL VERBS
128–136

TESTS 137–147

ANSWER KEY 148–162

INDEX 163–168

To the student

Grammar Practice for Intermediate Students gives short, clear explanations of all the main areas of English grammar, and provides practice exercises for you to do. There are two ways in which this book can be used;

(i) in class with help from your teacher;
(ii) at home by yourself.

If you are using the book by yourself, use the Index and the Contents list to find the areas that you want to study, read the grammatical explanation, and then do the exercise. To check your answers you will need to use the edition of *Grammar Practice for Intermediate Students with Answer key*.

We hope that *Grammar Practice for Intermediate Students* helps you to improve your English.

Elaine Walker
Steve Elsworth

Nouns and adjectives

1 The articles *a* and *the*

- *a* is used:
  - a) with countable nouns to indicate *one*:
    *I've got **a** cat.*
  - b) to indicate cost, speed, or frequency:
    *fifty pence **a** kilo*
    *four times **a** day*
    *two hundred kilometres **an** hour*
  - c) for certain numbers:
    ***a** hundred; **a** thousand; **a** couple; **a** dozen*

- *the* is used:
  - a) when a word is used a second time *(cuando sabemos de lo que estamos hablando)*
  - b) when talking about a known object:
    *I've just washed **the** car.* (= our car, or this car)
    *Where's **the** dog?* (= our dog, or the dog that is usually here)
    *We've made **the** beds.* (= our beds, or the beds here)
  - c) in a general sense, with musical instruments:
    *Can you play **the** guitar?*

    *I like listening to **the** piano.*
    Note: *I've just bought **a** guitar and **a** piano.* *(Acabo de comprar una guitarra y un piano)*
  - d) when the object is unique:
    ***the** moon.* More important!!

- Usually, no article is used:
  - a) with abstract nouns (*life, beauty, love,* etc.), languages, and academic subjects (*history, Latin,* etc.):
    Life isn't always easy.
    Latin is a difficult language to learn.
  - b) with materials (*wine, coal, sugar,* etc.) when they are considered in a general sense:
    Glass is a difficult material to cut.
    Gold is very expensive at the moment.
    Note: There is a difference between:
    They were looking for gold. (= any gold)
    *They found **the** gold.* (= the gold they were looking for)
  - c) before countries and towns:
    They live in Manchester.
  - d) before *school, home, work, church, bed,* and *hospital* in certain expressions:
    We went to church.
    She's at home.

* Cuando es general no se pone (el artículo) cuando es específico sí Delante de lo edificios no se pone art.

1

Practice

Write *a*, *the*, or no article to complete these sentences.

1 She's a good musician: she plays *the* piano beautifully.

2 I don't see him often, only once or twice ..*a*... month.

3 Mary's not at *the* office. I think she's gone ..—... home.

4 Do you want to see Sarah? She's in *the* garden.

5 I'm studying ..—... French and ..—..., Italian.

6 I like Jane, she has a lot of ..—... warmth.

7 Shall we sit outside? *The* sun is really warm.

8 Where's ..*the*. dog? I want to go out for ...*a*... walk.

9 I don't use ..—... sugar when I'm cooking.

10 Do your parents still live in ..—... Scotland?

11 Would you mind waiting for ..*a*... couple of minutes?

12 I think ..*the* piano is one of the easiest instruments to play.

13 It's ..*a*... fast car. Its top speed is 150 miles ..*an*... hour.

14 I saw her when she was going to ..—... work.

15 There's someone at *the* front door.

16 Do you like ..—... wine? No, I don't drink ..—... alcohol.

17 I'll have ..*a*... dozen eggs and ..*a*... loaf, please.

18 Coal is sixty dollars ..*the*... ton at the moment.

19 Have you done ..*the*... washing-up?

20 I think it's made of ..—... glass.

21 I like ..—... tea with ..—... milk in it.

22 I stayed at home last night and listened to *the* radio.

23 Would you like ..*a*... cup of coffee?

24 They gave me ..*a*... diamond necklace.

25 When he was nineteen, he joined ..*the*. army.

2   Words using *a*, *the*, or no article

- Some words are used with *a*, *the*, or no article, depending on the meaning of the word, and whether it is thought of as definite (*the*), indefinite (*a*), or uncountable:

  *I put **the** glass on the table.* (definite – a particular glass)
  *I picked up **a** glass.* (indefinite – one of a number of glasses)
  It's made of glass. (uncountable – glass as material)

Practice

Write *a, the,* or no article to complete these sentences.

> tin

1 Could I have ten eggs and ..a.. tin of peas? _plata_

2 Put some money in *the* tin by the door when you leave, please.

3 The cigarette lighter's made of ..—.. tin.

> wood

4 We knew that ..—.... wood was a very expensive material at the time.

5 There's ..a.... wood at the end of the road.

6 There are some rabbits living at the edge of .*the*.. wood. _extremo_

> paper

7 The boy who delivers ..*the*... paper is late today.

8 It was very strange, a shirt made of ..—..... paper.

9 I generally read ...a... paper of some sort on the train. _cualquier tipo_

> chocolate

10 I won't take ..a..... chocolate, thanks, although they look very nice. _alguna_

11 Most doctors say ..—..... chocolate is bad for you.

12 *The*.. chocolates which I ate last night tasted very strange.

> dress

13 She has a good sense of ..—..... dress.

14 *The*.. dress I liked was a bit too big for me.

15 I saw ...a.... beautiful dress here yesterday

> experience

16 I'm afraid I didn't enjoy ..*the*. experience at all.

17 For this job you need ..—..... experience with computers.

18 My first trip abroad was ..a.... wonderful experience.

> noise

19 I couldn't hear her because of .*the*. noise on the train.

20 She heard ...a.... strange noise behind the curtain. _cortinas_

21 What kind of ..—.... noise are you talking about?

3   *a, the*, or no article

Practice

Circle the correct answer.

I could tell by (*a*/*the*/-) town hall clock that I was late, so I decided to catch (*a*/-) bus. It was (*a*/*the*/-) beautiful day; (*a*/*the*/-) sun was shining and there was (*the*/-) very little wind. I turned (*the*/-) corner, and walked down (*a*/*the*/-) main street.

(*A*/*the*/-) couple of minutes later, I heard (*a*/*the*/-) noise, and (*a*/*the*/-) man wearing (*a*/*the*/-) grey leather jacket ran past me. At first, I thought he was trying to catch (*the*/-) bus which was waiting at (*the*/-) bus stop, but then (*a*/*the*/-) policeman appeared, running at (*a*/-) some speed. He was obviously chasing (*a*/*the*/-) man in (*a*/*the*/-) leather jacket, and he was joined by another policeman, who was talking rapidly into (*a*/*the*/-) hand-held radio. All three disappeared into (*a*/-) crowd of people, my bus arrived, and I got on. As (*a*/*the*/-) bus drove down (*the*/-) road, I saw (*a*/*the*/-) man again, walking casually through (*a*/*the*/-) crowd with his (*the*/-) coat over his shoulder. I could also see (*a*/*the*/-) second policeman, still talking into his radio. He was describing (*a*/-) man who no longer existed, (*a*/-) man wearing a jacket and running furiously: while (*a*/*the*/-) real criminal (if he was (*a*/-) criminal) walked slowly and casually into the station.

4   Possessives with *'s, s'* and *of*

- To indicate possession for people or animals:
  a) add *'s* to singular nouns, and to plural nouns not ending in *s*:
     Monica's dress
     the dog's nose
     the children's school
  b) add *'* to plural nouns ending in *s*:
     dolphins' brains
     the sailors' hats

- To indicate possession for things:
  a) use *of*:
  the end *of* the road
  the smell *of* cooking
  the leader *of* the party
  b) for common nouns (*house, car, school, table*, etc.) *of* is not necessary, and the word position changes:
  car keys
  the kitchen door
  a bus driver
  c) always use *of* with the words *front, top, bottom, back, end*:
  the bottom *of* the garden (NOT ~~the garden bottom~~)
  the front *of* the house (NOT ~~the house front~~)
  d) for expressions of time, *'s* or *s'* is used:
  a fortnight*'s* holiday
  two weeks*'* rest

Practice

Use the correct possessives to complete the sentences. If two answers are possible, write the more likely one.

1 Where are the *boys' books*? (books/boys)

2 I opened the *car door* . (door/car)

3 My keys are in the *pocket of my suit* . (pocket/my suit)

4 She closed the ...*kitchen door*... . (door/kitchen)

5 The ...*men's clothes*... were old and dirty. (clothes/men)

6 She put her suitcase in the ...*car boot*... . (boot/car)

7 My room is at the ...*front of the hotel*... (front/hotel)

8 She's been studying ...*chimpanzees' behaviour*... for 20 years. (behaviour/chimpanzees)

9 We sat on the ...*sitting-room carpet*... (carpet/sitting-room)

10 I'm afraid I've broken the ...*leg of the chair*... . (leg/chair)

11 The doctor told me to have a ...*week's rest*... (rest/week)

12 He wrote a letter to the ...*president's secretary*... . (secretary/President)

13 Would you turn on the ...*kitchen light*...? (light/kitchen)

14 Someone has damaged the ...*front of my car*... . (front/my car)

15 This is Mrs Davies, the ...*cinema manager*... . (manager/cinema)

16 The cat walked along the ...*garden wall*... . (wall/garden)

17 You'll feel better after a ...*fortnight's holiday*... .
(holiday/fortnight) [15 días]

18 Could someone open the ...*window of the bathroom*...
(window/bathroom) → *bathroom window*

19 After ...*three hours' delay*... the plane took off. (delay/three
hours)

20 This was ...*my parents' house*... (house/my parents)

5   Singular and plural

- To make singular words plural, add **s**.
  a) If the word ends in **o** or **s**, add **es**:
    tomato → tomatoes; glass → glasses.

    Note the exceptions: *piano → pianos; stereo → stereos; disco → discos; video → videos.*

- b) If the word is **half, leaf, thief, self, shelf, wife, wolf,** or **knife,** change the **f**
  or **fe** to **ves**:
    half → halves; wolf → wolves.

    Note that most other words ending in **f** just add **s**: *roof → roofs.*

- c) Some animals have the same form in singular and plural:
    deer → deer; sheep → sheep; fish → fish (or *fishes*)

    Note: the plural of **mouse** is **mice**.

Notes

- If the words ends in **ch, sh, x** or **s**, add **es**:
  match → matches; box → boxes
- If the word ends in **y**, change to **ies**:
  baby → babies; lady → ladies
- Remember the common irregular plurals:
  men, women, children, people, teeth, feet

Practice

Write the plurals of the words given in brackets to complete these sentences.

1 Would you bring the bottle and some .*glasses*., please? (glass)

2 We cut the cake into ...*halves*... . (half)

3 We bought some ...*tomatoes*... to eat with our .*sandwiches*. .
(tomato/sandwich)

4 They caught several ...*fishes*... that afternoon. (fish)

5 It was a shop selling ...*stereos*... and ...*videos*... .
(stereo/video)

6 Would you like some of these ...*potatoes*...? (potato)

7   We saw a cartoon about ..... cats .... and .... mice ....
    (cat/mouse)

8   All the ..... houses .... had different coloured .... roofs ....
    (house/roof)

9   It was autumn, and the ...... leaves .... were falling. (leaf)   *hoja*

10 Did you make these ... handkerchieves? (handkerchief) *pañuelo de bolsillo.*

11 We use several ...... processes .... for painting the
    .... cars .... (process/car)

12 They have some ..... chickens .... and a few .. sheeps ....
    (chicken/sheep)

13 They visited several ...... discos .... that night. (disco)

14 I've read her ...... books ...., but I haven't seen any of her
    .... plaies .... (book/play)

15 I bought some .. shelves .... for the ... glasses ....
    (shelf/glass)

16 There were .... thousands .. of .. boxes .... in the factory.
    (thousand/box)

17 The ..... men .... went in one door and the .. women ....
    went in the other. (man/woman)

18 They have a lot of .... worries .... at the moment. (worry)

19 Would you bring the .... knives .... and ... forks ....?
    (knife/fork)

20 The ... wolves ...... chased the ... deers .... for several
    miles. (wolf/deer)

6   Comparatives and superlatives

FORM

	Comparative	Superlative
One-syllable adjectives	older, faster	oldest, fastest
One-syllable adjectives ending in -*e*	wider, nicer	widest, nicest
One-syllable adjectives ending in one vowel + consonant	hottest, biggest	hotter, bigger
Two-syllable adjectives ending in -*y*, -*er*, -*ow*	happier, funnier, cleverer, narrower	happiest, funniest, cleverest, narrowest
Other adjectives with two or more syllables	more careful, more interesting	most careful, most interesting
Irregular adjectives: good, bad, little	better, worse, less	best worst, least

USE

- Comparatives are used to compare two nouns. They are followed by **than** if the second noun is mentioned:
  *Cats are **cleverer than** dogs, but dogs are **friendlier**.*
- Superlatives are used to compare one thing with more than one other thing. They are used with **the**:
  *John is **the youngest** child in the class.*

Practice

Write the comparative or superlative of the adjectives in brackets.

1   It's *warmer* today than it was yesterday. (warm)

2   This is the *most expensive* dress in the shop. (expensive)

3   What's the .... mountain in your country? (high)

4   This car is too small. We need to get a .... one. (big)

5   It was the .... music I've ever heard. (beautiful)

6   Your computer is .... than mine. (modern)

7   Australia is the earth's .... continent. (old)

8   My sister was always .... than me. (pretty)

9   This year's exam was .... than last year's. (difficult)

10 This is the .... pan we've got. (large)

7 The qualification of comparatives and superlatives

The chair is	a bit a little a little bit much quite a lot a lot	cheaper more comfortable	than that one.

This chair is	as nearly as n't as n't nearly as twice/three times as	cheap comfortable	as that one.

It's	by far easily	the most expensive car in the world. the most expensive of all the cars I've seen.

Practice

Complete these sentences.

1 the weather is much _warmer than_ it usually is at this time. (warm)

2 Going by car took twice _as long as_ going by train. (long)

3 It was by far _the worst_ time of my life. (bad)

4 The train's a lot .... all the other ways of getting there. (fast)

5 This exam was a bit .... all the other tests. (easy)

6 I think English spelling is by far .... (difficult)

7 The food isn't nearly .... it has been in the past. (good)

8 She's a bit .... her brother. (sensitive)

9 Flying's a lot .... going by car. (quick)

10 First class is much .... second. (expensive)

11 This is easily .... restaurant in London. (good)

12 Ellen was a bit .... she usually is. (cheerful)

13 He's not nearly .... his sister. (intelligent)

14 The journey was three times .... we had expected.
   (long)

15 The film wasn't .... I had thought it would be.
   (good)

8   *so* and *such*

So and **such** are used to strengthen the meaning of adjectives and adverbs.

• **such** is used before an adjective that comes before a noun:
  *She was **such** a good actress.*
  *It's **such** a cold day, isn't it?*

  Note: **such** + [*a/an*] + adjective + noun (singular or plural)
  He shouldn't buy such expensive clothes.

• **so** is used before an adjective alone or an adverb:
  *You look **so** lovely!*
  *He dresses **so** badly.*

• **so** and **such** are often used with *that*-clauses to talk about the result or
  consequence of something:
  It's such a stupid idea that I don't think we should consider it.
  (It's a very stupid idea. For that reason, I don't think we should consider it.)
  I was so tired that I fell asleep in the lecture.
  (I was very tired. For that reason, I fell asleep in the lecture.)

Practice

Write **so** or **such** to complete these sentences.

1 It was *such* terrible weather that we had to stay at home.

2 She spoke *so* clearly that I understood everything.

3 You should read this book – it's .... interesting.

4 There was .... a long queue that I decided not to wait.

5 She's .... a good doctor that I'm sure you'll be happy with her.

6 That man is driving .... slowly that I'm going to overtake.

7 That decision was .... a terrible mistake.

8 He worked .... hard that he had a nervous breakdown.

9 It's .... difficult to decide what to do.

10 He committed .... a serious crime that he ought to stay in prison for
   life.

Verbs

THE PRESENT TENSE

9   Present Simple and Present Continuous

Present simple

FORM

REMEMBER!

I/You/We/They eat; He/She/It eats.   *I/You/We/They do not (don't) eat.*
Do I/You/he/she/it/we/they eat?   *He/She/It does not (doesn't) eat.*

Note the endings with *he*, *she*, and *it*. If the verb ends in *ss*, *sh*, *ch*, or *x*, add *es*:
He washes (*wash* ends in *sh*)
She catches (*catch* ends in *ch*)

USE

• for something that is permanently true:
  She comes from Argentina.
  I don't speak Chinese.
• for habits and repeated actions:
  How often do you go to the gym?
  He usually leaves work at 6 o'clock.

Present continuous

FORM

Positive

I	am → I'm	
He She It	is → He's She's It's	working.
We You They	are → We're You're They're	

Question

Am	I	
Is	he she it	working?
Are	we you they	

Negative with **not**

I	am → I'm	
He She It	is → He's She's It's	not working.
We You They	are → We're You're They're	

Negative with **n't**

–		
He She It	isn't	working.
We You They	aren't	

USE

- For an action in progress now:
  Are you waiting for the bus?
  I'm writing a letter to Julie.

Practice

Complete these sentences, putting the verbs into the correct tense.

1 What's that book you .'re reading.? (read)

2 We usually .go.. to the beach at the weekend. (go)

3 She .... to me every week. (write)

4 'Where's Kevin?'

   'He .... football with his friends.' (play)

5 My boss .... to New York every month. (fly)

6 Can you answer the phone? I .... (cook)

7 Look! That man .... to get into our car. (try)

8 .... to school every morning? (you walk)

9 The bank .... on Sundays. (not open)

10 Her son .... her very often. (not visit)

11 He .... his car every weekend. (wash)

12 Sorry, you can't talk to him. He .... a shower. (have)

13 'What .... ?'

   'My homework.' (do)

14 Snakes .... for most of the day. (sleep)

15 Many people .... this kind of food. (not like)

16 'Could you be quiet, please – I .... the radio.' (listen)

17 We .... in a hotel at the moment. (stay)

18 She .... to work by train. (go)

19 They never .... to me. (write)

20 I .... for Mary. She's late. (wait)

10   Verbs using Present Simple rather than Present Continuous

USE

- Certain verbs generally use only the simple form, and are not used with the continuous. These are verbs which do not describe activities. They include:
  a) verbs of thinking and understanding:
  *I **believe** you.*
  *I don't **understand**.*
  *What do you **think**?*
  b) verbs of seeing, hearing, feeling, etc.:
  *I don't **like** him.*
  *How do you **feel**?*
  *I **want** to go.*

- These verbs can use the present continuous when they become activity verbs:
  *Be quiet, please: I'm **thinking**.* (Here ***thinking*** is an activity, like ***working***.)
  *I'm **seeing** the president tomorrow.* (***seeing*** = ***meeting***)

- There is a difference between these verbs:
  listen – hear; watch – see; look – see
  Listen, watch and ***look*** are deliberate activities, and can use the present continuous:
  *I'm **listening** to the radio.*
  Hear and ***see*** are not deliberate activities, and do not usually use the continuous.

➤ Exercise 66 for an explanation of simple and continuous aspects.

Practice

Circle the correct form of the verb in these sentences.

1   You're very quiet. What (*do you think* / *are you thinking*) about?

2   What (*are you thinking* / *do you think*) about the new sports centre?

3   I'm sorry (*I'm not agreeing* / *I don't agree*) with you.

4   (*Are you looking* / *Do you look*) for me?

5   (*Do you prefer* / *Are you preferring*) walking to cycling?

6   (*I don't like* / *I'm not liking*) him at the moment.

7   (*I hear* / *I'm hearing*) you're leaving us.

8   I'm afraid (*I'm not remembering* / *I don't remember*) where we met.

9   (*Do you listen* / *Are you listening*) to the radio at the moment?

10 (*I'm hating* / *I hate*) cold evenings.

11 (*I'm not looking forward* / *I don't look forward*) to my holiday.

12 (*They're looking* / *They look*) at clothes at the moment.

13 Why (*aren't you agreeing* / *don't you agree*) with the idea?

14 What (*is this meaning?* / *does this mean?*)

15 (*I'm not understanding* / *I don't understand*) the lessons.

16 (*I never agree* / *I'm never agreeing*) with what he says.

17 (*He knows* / *He's knowing*) you're wrong.

18 (*They watch* / *They're watching*) us.

11 Present Simple and Present Continuous: permanent and temporary

CONTRAST

* The present simple is used to express permanent facts.

* The present continuous is sometimes used as a contrast to the present simple, to show temporary events:
  *I **live** in Mexico, though I**'m staying** in Texas at the moment.*
  *I**'m living** in Paris just now, but I **come** from Belgium.*

Practice

Complete these sentences, putting the verbs into the correct tense.

1 I *live* in Washington, though I*'m staying* in London at the moment.

2 The car isn't here today because Sheila (use) .... it. She generally (use) .... the bus, but the drivers are on strike.

3 We usually (stay) .... at home on Fridays, but we came out tonight because we (celebrate) .... our anniversary.

4 I (come) .... from Scotland, though I (live) .... in London just now.

5 I (stay) .... with my parents at the moment, though I (have) .... my own flat.

6 They usually (work) .... at the weekends, though they (not work) .... at the moment.

7 He (teach) .... in a language school, though he (work) .... in a factory at the moment because the school's on holiday.

8 The business usually (make) .... money, though it (do) .... rather badly just now.

9 I usually (work) .... at night, though I (have) .... a holiday at the moment.

10 I (study) .... French at the moment, but I (not speak) .... it very well yet.

THE PAST

12 Past Simple and Past Continuous

Past simple

FORM

REMEMBER!

Positive   *Question*   *Negative*
She play**ed**   **Did** she play?   She **didn't** play.

- For irregular verb forms, see Exercise 29.

USE

- For a completed action or state in the past. (pasado)
  I saw a great film last night.
  We lived in Sydney for two years.

Past continuous

FORM

REMEMBER!

I/He/She/It was running.
We/You/They were running.
Was I/he/she/it running?
Were we/you/they running?
I/He/She/It was not (wasn't) running.
We/You/They were not (weren't) running.

USE

- To describe a past action at some point between its beginning and its end:
  At 8 o'clock last night we were having dinner.
  He was walking down the road when he heard a loud noise.
  calle abajo

Practice

Complete these sentences by putting the verbs into the past simple or the past continuous.

1   Do you like this picture? My uncle *painted* it. (paint)

2   We *were having* lunch when we heard the news. (have)

3   He broke his arm when he *was playing* rugby. (play)

4   Kylie *made* her first film when she was 21. (make)

5   *Did you see* the football match yesterday? (you see)

6   I *was working* on the computer when the earthquake happened. (work)

7   Who was that man you *were talking* to when I came in? (talk)

8   She was so tired that she *slept* for twelve hours. (sleep)

9 The fire ....destroyed..... the old church completely. (destroy)

10 I ...was waiting........... in the queue when the robber came in. (wait)

11 I ....was having........... a bath when she phoned. (have)

12 They .....knocked..... on the door, then they went in. (knock)

13 Mark and Theresa .....lived.............. in Poland for many years. (live)

14 The police .....asked............. them lots of questions before they
    released them. (ask)

15 We .....were having........... tea when they arrived. (have)

16 What ...were you doing... when the alarm sounded? (you do)

17 The factory ....made............. six thousand cars last year. (make)

18 She ...didn't say..... anything to my parents. (not say)

19 James .....was walking....... through the forest when the storm started.
    (walk)

13 Past continuous as narrative

The past continuous is often used in a past simple narrative to describe the background history or environment:

It was a typical summer afternoon: the sun **was beating** down, the cars **were creeping** slowly round the corner of the park. Five or six children **were playing** in the stream by the fountain, jumping in and out of the water, their laughter mixing with the noise of the traffic. All the world **was wearing** shorts and T-shirts, or bathing costumes: yet Walter Harrison, sitting on a park bench in his overcoat, **was feeling** cold and lonely. 'Where will it all end?' he thought, as he watched the children splashing and laughing. After a few minutes, he got up and walked through the park gates. His adventure was about to begin ...

Practice

In your notebook, write the verbs in this story in the past simple or past continuous. Sometimes both tenses are possible. Choose the one that is most likely.

He stopped just before putting his key in the front door. Something was happening in the back garden. Quietly, he crept around the side of the house and [1](*look*) through the gate. Two men [2](*stand*) at the back of the house, holding a ladder. A third man was at the top of the ladder, and a fourth inside the house: he [3](*pass*) furniture through the window to his partner, who [4](*give*) it to his friends below. All four [5](*work*) quietly and efficiently, and the pile of furniture in the garden [6](*get*) bigger by the minute. Derek [7](*can not*) believe his eyes: the team of strangers [8](*empty*) his entire flat, and they [9](*behave*) as if this was the most normal thing in the world! He [10](*cough*) loudly, and then [11](*say*) 'Excuse me!' – and the man at the top of the ladder [12](*drop*) his portable TV onto the concrete below.

➤ Exercise 27 for an explanation of the simple and continuous aspects.

14   Present Perfect

FORM

| **has/have** + past participle |

REMEMBER!

I/You/We/They have ('ve) finished.
He/She/It has ('s) finished.
Have I/we/you/they finished?
Has he/she/it finished?
I/We/You/They have not (haven't) finished.
He/She/It has not (hasn't) finished.

USE

The present perfect is used to show a connection in the speaker's mind between the past and the present. This occurs in two main ways.

a) the unfinished past:

He's been here for 10 minutes. (and he is still here now)
We've lived here since 1996. (and we still live here now)
I've written three letters today.
She's travelled to six countries since she started the job.

b) the indefinite past:

I've broken a glass.
John has lost his job.
I've just heard the news. ⟹ Acabo de escuchar la noticia.
Have you finished that report yet?
Have you ever been to China? ⟹ Has estado en china?
She's never flown in a plane.
She's the best teacher I've ever had.

Practice

Choose the correct response from the following page.

1   Do you know your neighbours well? .....n....

2   I'd like to speak to Mr Jones, please. ....c......

3   You look tired. ...g.....

4   What's the matter? ....o.....

5   Shall we cycle into town? .....a....

6   Have you ever been to London? ..m.....

7   You're looking very happy. ...k.....

8   Can't you go a little bit faster? ....l......

9   Do you like skiing? .....f.....

10   Why don't you come out with us tonight? ...e.....

11   We ought to book our flight. ....h.....

12   What do you think of my essay? .....j.....

13   Do you know where Sarah is? ....b.....

14   Did you enjoy New Zealand?   ...f.......

15   Why isn't Andrew at work today?   ..d......

a)   I'm afraid I can't. Isabel's borrowed my bike for the weekend.

b)   No. I haven't seen her since she went out this morning.

c)   I'm sorry. He's just left the office.

d)   He's hurt his back so he's gone to see the doctor.

e)   I've been out every night this week and I'm exhausted.

f)   Yes. It's the most beautiful country I've ever been to.

g)   That's because we've walked 30 kilometres today.

h)   Don't worry. I've already done it.

i)   I'm sorry. This is the first time I've driven this car.

j)   I don't know. I haven't read it yet.

k)   Yes. I've just heard that I've passed my exams.

l)   I've never tried it.

m)   No, I haven't. Have you?

n)   Yes. They've lived here for ten years.

o)   I've cut my finger.

15   Past Simple and Present Perfect

Practice

In your notebook, write the story, putting the verbs in brackets into the present perfect or past simple. If two answers are possible, write the more likely one.

Ann Jones is one of the most interesting people I [1](*meet*): she is only twenty-five, but she [2](*travel*) to over fifty different countries. Five years ago, she [3](*be*) a typist in Birmingham, but she [4](*decide*) to give up her job and see the world. Since then, her life [5](*change*) completely.

The first time she [6](*go*) abroad was seven years ago, when she [7](*be*) just eighteen. She [8](*take*) a boat to France and then [9](*hitch-hike*) around Europe for five weeks. She [10](*visit*) Europe many times since that first trip, of course, but this holiday [11](*be*) the one which [12](*make*) her start travelling. She [13](*never forget*) the excitement of those five weeks – although it [14](*be*) not all enjoyable. When she [15](*be*) on a train, somebody [16](*steal*) her purse: she [17](*lose*) all her money, and [18](*have*) to work in a restaurant for a fortnight. She [19](*make*) some good friends there, however, and [20](*return*) several times since then.

How did she find the money for her travels? After her first trip abroad, she [21](*go*) home and [22](*work*) for two years, saving all the time. Now she travels continually, finding work when her money gets low. She [23](*make*) a lot of friends, she says, and [24](*learn*) quite a few languages. Although she [25](*have*) occasional difficulties and [26](*often be*) sick, she [27](*never think*) about giving up her travels. 'The first time I [28](*go*) abroad [29](*change*) my life,' she says, 'and I [30](*want*) to travel ever since.'

16   Present Perfect Continuous

FORM

has/have + been + *verb* -ing

CONTRAST with present perfect simple

- The present perfect simple is used when the action is complete and the final achievement is important:
  I've run six kilometres.
  (NOT *I've been running six kilometres.*)

- The present perfect continuous is used when the activity is important. We are interested in how someone has been spending time, and the achievement is not important:
  I've been running. (NOT *I've run.*)

Practice

In your notebook, write the dialogue, putting the verbs into the present perfect simple or continuous as necessary.

JULIA: Gosh, it ¹(*be*) busy this morning, hasn't it?

PAT: Yes, you look exhausted. What ²(*you do*)?

JULIA: I ³(*not stop*) all morning. I ⁴(*write*) letters, ⁵(*answer*) the phone, ⁶(*do*) the filing … it ⁷(*be*) impossible!

PAT: It ⁸(*be*) the same for me. My phone ⁹(*ring*) all morning, I ¹⁰(*write*) five letters … and I ¹¹(*interview*) three people for that secretarial job.

JULIA: Have you? Oh, I ¹²(*interview*) one as well. And I ¹³(*send*) off another ten application forms to people who want them. It seems to be very popular.

PAT: It does, doesn't it? I can't think why. Four people ¹⁴(*phone*) me about it this morning.

JULIA: Have they? Oh, and I ¹⁵(*look*) through that letter, you know, the one the managing director sent to all the staff …

PAT: Oh, yes, I ¹⁶(*already read*) that. Not very interesting, is it?

JULIA: No … I think I ¹⁷(*read*) it all before …

17 Past Perfect

FORM

| had/'d + past participle |

USE

- To describe the first of two events in the past:
  I **had spoken** to Mr Johnson before the meeting began.

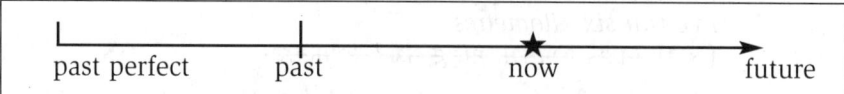

- To describe a period of time leading up to a time in the past:
  By 1984, we **had waited** seven years for an answer.

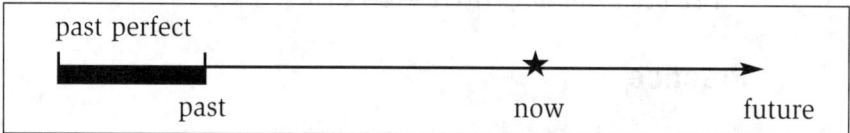

Note the difference between past simple + past simple:
  I **got** to the stadium at 7.15, and the game **started** at 7.30.
  (= the game started **after** I arrived)
  and past simple + past perfect:
  I **got** to the stadium at 7.45, and the game **had started** at 7.30.
  (= the game started **before** I arrived)

Practice

Write the sentences, putting one verb in each sentence into the past simple, and the other verb into the past perfect.

1 When the police (arrive), the car (go).

   When the police arrived, the car had gone.

2 When I (get) to the shop, it (close).

   ....

3 They (eat) everything by the time I (arrive) at the party.

   ....

   ....

4 When we (leave) the beach, the rain (already start).

   ....

   ....

5 I (try) telephoning her several times but she (leave the country).

   ....

   ....

6 When I (find) my purse, someone (take) the money out of it.

....

....

7 The car (go) when I (look) into the street.

....

....

8 The patient (already die) by the time I (see) her.

....

....

9 All the garages (close) by the time we (cross) the border.

....

....

10 (You already leave) when the trouble (start)?

....

....

11 The post (not arrive) when I (leave) the house this morning.

....

....

12 By the time I get) into town, the shops (close).

....

....

18 Past Perfect Continuous

FORM

> **had/'d** + **been** + verb-**ing**

USE

- As present perfect continuous, but changed because it occurs in a past narrative:
  *She's **been working** all night.* ➜ *When I got there, she **had been working** all night.*
  *They've **been living** there for years.* ➜ *They didn't like the house, even though they **had been living** there for years.*
  *She's **been reading** for hours.* ➜ *There were books everywhere: she **had been reading** for hours.*

Practice

This is part of a newspaper story written in 1990. Rewrite it in your notebook, putting the verbs into the past perfect or past simple. Start your story with the words:

By 1999, Mr and Mrs Charlton had been living in Portland Street for ...

Mr and Mrs Charlton have been living in Portland Street for five years. They have tried to move several times, but this has not been possible, as they are unable to sell their house. Several people have looked at the property, but quickly lost interest – and the reason for this is obvious. For three years the garden of 17 Portland Street has been covered by three feet of water. The Charltons tried to find the reason for this strange occurrence, but no one has been able to help. The water level has been rising since 1996, and has damaged the whole of the ground floor. The Charltons have been keeping the water back with sandbags, but of course this is only a temporary defence. Mrs Charlton says she has contacted the water authorities, the town council, even her local MP, but no one has been able to explain why their back garden has become a swimming pool for all the children in the neighbourhood.

19   Present, Past, Present Perfect

Check

Write the verbs in the correct tense.

1   She paid for her ticket and .... (leave)

2   I closed the door quietly because he .... to sleep. (try)

3   How many times .... since he came to New York? (she call)

4   I .... about this for some time now. (know)

5   They .... television – their favourite programme is on at the moment. (watch)

6   I wanted to be the first to tell her the news, but it was too late. Someone .... her. (already tell)

7   The children are filthy. Where ....? (they be)

8   I'm going to bed. I .... for hours and I'm tired. (work)

9   I think she's the nicest person I .... (ever meet)

10   Mary was cleaning the windscreen when she .... a crack in the glass. (notice)

11 I couldn't open the office door because someone

.... it. (lock)

12 I agree: I .... you should apologize. (not think)

13 When I phoned her, she .... her homework.

(do)

14 We .... for three-and-a-half hours when John

finally arrived. (wait)

15 When I shouted, they .... off the roof and

.... away. (jump/run)

16 Don't phone her just now. She .... to her

boss. (talk)

17 Oh! You .... a shave! You look strange

without a beard! (have)

18 I .... military service for eighteen months.

This is my last month. (do)

19 We .... for about four hours when we

realized that something was wrong with one of the tyres. (travel)

20 Mary will be ready soon. She .... a bath at

the moment. (have)

21 Sorry, I .... Could you say that again please?

(not understand)

22 We .... in the cafe until the rain stopped and

then went home. (stay)

23 .... here before? (you be)

24 There was nobody at the office. Mr Brownlow

.... the staff to go home. (tell)

25 I signed the register and .... upstairs to my

room. (go)

26 He had been working in the garden, but he

.... when he saw us. (stop)

27 I couldn't drive to work because Mary ....

the car. (use)

28 How many times .... him since he went to

Edinburgh? (you see)

29 Peter and Jane ....: I could here them from my room. (argue)

30 I .... him since he started working here. (never trust)

31 I'm worried. Why .... yet? (they not arrive)

32 They're very angry. They .... to see you for the last two or three hours. (try)

33 I wanted to help with the washing-up, but they .... it. (already do)

34 It's the most comfortable car I .... (ever drive)

35 Peter was cleaning the flat and John .... (the dinner)

36 I had a pleasant surprise when I got to my room: someone .... some flowers there for me. (put)

37 .... that we should tell him tomorrow? (you agree)

38 They couldn't leave the studio when I called because they .... a film. (edit)

39 I .... the machine for some time when I realised that there was no ink in it. (use)

40 When he warned them about the police, they .... the country. (leave)

41 Don't make a noise: the children .... to sleep. (try)

42 Oh! You .... a new dress! (buy)

43 She .... here for several years – four or five now, I think. (work)

44 We .... in the sunshine for about twenty-five minutes when I suddenly felt sick. (sit)

45 He'll be ready in a moment. He .... his shoes. (clean)

46 I .... listening to their complaints all day. One of these days I'll tell them what I really think. (hate)

47 I .... down on the bed and fell asleep. (lie)

48 I think I .... him somewhere before. (see)

49 I couldn't get into the car, because the children

.... the car keys. (hide)

50 Peter was meeting someone that night, so I

.... at the office and

.... for a few hours. (stay/work)

THE FUTURE

20 Present Continuous, *going to,* and Future Simple

REMEMBER!

USE

Present continuous as future
- A planned future action:
  I'm seeing Jessica tonight.

'*Going to*' future
- Planned future events:
  They're going to open the new offices on 1st March.

- Future events evident from something in the present:
  Look at the snow. It's going to be difficult to get into work tomorrow.

- Future events in a neutral way:
  Richard's going to be the new director.

Future Simple
- Statements of future fact:
  The job will be finished by the weekend.

- Decisions made at the time of speaking:
  There's Eleanor. I'll go and talk to her.

- To show willingness:
  I'll help you.

Practice

Write the following sentences in the most likely form (present continuous, *going to*, or future simple).

1 'We've run out of milk.'

   'Oh, have we? I *'ll go* and get some.' (go)

2 'So you've moved into your new house. Congratulations!'

   'Thank you. We *'re going to have* a party soon.' (have)

3 I'm afraid I can't come to dinner on Saturday – I 'm meeting
   Tim. (meet)

4 Josh will be five next Tuesday. (be)

5 It's raining – we 'll have to take an umbrella. (have to)

6 My cousins are coming to stay with us at the weekend.
   (come)

7 Look at that car! It is going to hit that tree! (hit)

8 I promise I am dond t go to that again. (not do)

9 Did you hear that the company is going to open a new factory?
   (open)

10 You look tired. Sit down and I will make you a cup of tea.
    (make)

11 'I think there's someone at the door.' 'OK, I 'll go (go)
    and answer it.'

12 Are you going to stay (you/stay) at home this weekend?

13 Kate's really unhappy at work so she is going to look for (look for)
    a new job soon.

14 She looks really upset. I think she 'll cry (cry).

15 I know you've got a lot to do so I 'll try (try) and help
    you as much as I can.

16 What will you do (you/do) when you've spent all your
    money?

17 Kate phoned up. She is coming round (come round) to see us
    this afternoon.

18 I'm sorry I made you so angry. I won't do (not do)
    that again.

19 Look at the sky. It 's going to be (be) a lovely day today.

20 I'm sorry you're leaving. I hope you will come back (come
    back) and see us soon.

21　Present simple as future

'What time does our train leave?'
'The train leaves at eight, we arrive at Dover at twelve,
and get on the ferry an hour later.'

USE

• To describe an organized future timetable.

Practice

Do these sentences refer to the habitual present or the future? Circle P or F for each sentence.

1　I leave home at eight, walk to the station, and catch the 8.30 train. I always get to the office before nine. P/F

2　The committee leaves Stockholm on Sunday morning, arrives in Australia on Monday and starts work on Tuesday. P/F

3　Your plane leaves London at 8.30 and arrives in Cairo at 12.00. P/F

4　I travel by the 8.30 train because it gets to London before ten o'clock. P/F

5　You take the 1.30 train from Berlin which connects with the night ferry from the Hook of Holland. You arrive in London an hour before your appointment. P/F

6　I always take the night train from Edinburgh which arrives in London at half-past six. P/F

7　The hovercraft leaves Felixstowe at 12.00. It takes an hour, so you get there at 14.00 French time. P/F

8　The Prime Minister arrives in India on Tuesday, spends a couple of days in Delhi, then goes on to Malaysia. P/F

9　The local train is very slow and stops at all the stations between here and Peterborough. P/F

10　The bus leaves at four o'clock, we get to Dublin at seven, and we have to register at the hotel before half-past eight. P/F

22 Future Continuous

FORM

Positive			*Question*			*Negative*		
I He She It We You They	will ('ll)	be working.	Will	I he she it we you they	be working?	I He She It We You They	will not (won't)	be working.

USE

- To describe an action or event that will be in progress at some time in the future:

  *I'll **be waiting** at the station when you arrive.*
  *I'll **be watching** football at six.*

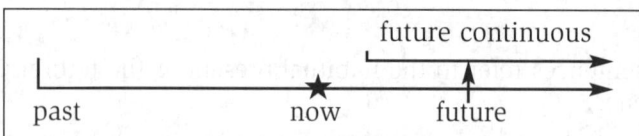

- To describe an activity or state that covers the whole of a future time period:

  *I'll **be watching** television all evening.*
  *I'll **be living** in London for the next few weeks.*

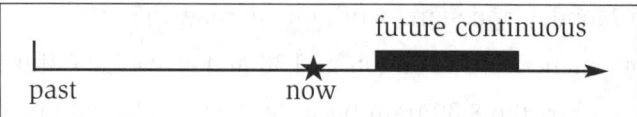

- To describe a future event which has already been arranged or is part of a regular routine.

  *I'll **be seeing** him tomorrow – I'll give him your note.*
  *I'll **be working** at home tomorrow – you can call me there.*

Notes

- *going to* or present continuous + time word can frequently be used instead of the future continuous. The main difference between the three is that ***going to*** and present continuous + time word usually refer to planned or intentional futures:

  *I'm **going to see** her tomorrow – we arranged it last week.*
  *I'm **seeing** her tomorrow, to talk about the new contract.*

  and the future continuous is less intentional:

  *I'll **be seeing** her tomorrow at the weekly sales conference: I'll talk to her about it then.*

- Future continuous is sometimes used to refer to the present, when we are guessing about what people are doing:

  *Peter and Tom **will be lying** on the beach in Corfu at the moment ....*
  *I bet they'll **be having** a good time now that it's hot.*
  *They'll probably **be staying** at an expensive hotel somewhere.*

Practice

Write the verbs below as future continuous or future simple.

1 I *'ll be seeing* (see) them tomorrow – I *'ll tell* (tell) them what you said.

2 *Will you be working* (you work) all tomorrow evening?

3 She .... (stay) in Leeds all weekend.

4 She .... (visit) our office next week – I
   .... (ask) her then.

5 I .... (see) the sales manager at the marketing
   meeting on Monday and I'm sure she .... (give) me
   the figures then.

6 I .... (not be able) to lend you the car – I
   .... (use) it all night.

7 Next year they .... (live) in Spain.

8 This time next week we .... (sit) on the beach.

9 The children .... (stay) with their grandparents for
   the summer holidays.

10 At four o'clock on Tuesday afternoon we .... (fly)
   over Paris.

11 What .... (you do) early on Monday night?

12 They .... (come) round for dinner tomorrow
   evening – I .... (show) them the photographs then.

13 He .... (arrive) in Paris now.

14 We .... (not hear) from him for some time – he
   .... (be) in Panama.

15 Don't phone them now: they .... (have) dinner.

23   Future Perfect

FORM
Simple

will/'ll + have + past participle

Positive

I He She It We You They	will ('ll)	have gone by 4 o'clock.

Question

Will	I he she it we you they	have gone by 4 o'clock?

Negative

I He She It We You They	will not (won't)	have gone by 4 o'clock.

Continuous

will/'ll + have been + *verb-ing*

Positive

I He She It We You They	will ('ll)	have been working here all day.

Question

Will	I he she it we you they	have been working here all day?

Negative

I He She It We You They	will not (won't)	have been working here all day.

USE

- Simple – to look ahead to a time in the future when:
  - a) an expected event or activity will be in the past:
    *I'll **have finished** work by five o'clock tonight.*
  - b) a duration of time will be in the past:
    *I'll **have been** here for a year in January.*

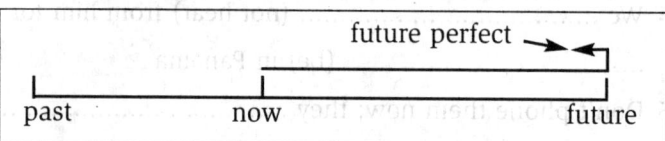

- Continuous
  - a) with **for**, to describe a period of time which precedes a point in the future.
    *We'll **have been living** here for two years in July.*
    (This can also be future perfect simple – see b) above)
  - b) to describe an activity which leads up to a point in the future:
    *I'll be dirty because I'll **have been playing** football.*

Practice

Write the verbs below in the future perfect simple or continuous. If two answers are possible, write the answer which you think is best for the sentences.

1 They'll probably be hungry because they *won't have eaten.* (not eaten)

2 I'll be tired tonight because I *'ll have been working* all day. (work)

3 I .... the entire committee by the time I leave England. (meet)

4 I .... for seven years when I get my degree. (study)

5 We .... here for six months by the time they find us a new flat. (live)

6 I .... for forty-five years by 2005. (work)

7 They .... in the cold for six hours by the time we pick them up. (stand)

8 Another million people .... unemployed by this time next year. (become)

9 She .... Prime Minister for ten years by next year. (be)

10 They .... for five hours by eight o'clock. (play)

11 We .... for two days by the time we get there. (drive)

12 They .... for twenty-four hours by twelve o'clock tomorrow. (not eat)

13 When they've talked to me, the police .... everybody in the office. (question)

14 She .... a member of the committee for twenty-five years by the time she retires. (be)

24   The future

Write the following sentences in the correct form (present simple, future
continuous, future perfect simple or future perfect continuous). If more than one
answer is possible, write the most likely once.

1   Next November we *'ll have been* married for fifteen years. (be)

2   What time *does the train leave?* (train leave)

3   Just think! This time next week we .... on

the beach! (lie)

4   I .... at the airport when your plane lands.

(wait)

5   In two weeks' time she .... her exams.

(finish)

6   .... Brian at the meeting? (you see)

7   At ten o'clock I .... for sixteen hours. (drive)

8   Hurry up! The lecture .... in five minutes.

(start)

9   By the end of the week we .... ten applicants

for the job. (interview)

10 Next time I write to you I .... in Australia.

(live)

25   Future in the past

FORM

> **was/were going to** + *infinitive*
> *I was going to leave early, but I didn't.*

USE

• to describe a planned action that did not happen:
  *I **was going to visit** my parents yesterday, but my car broke down.*
  *He **was going to say** something, but changed his mind.*
  *They **were going to stay** in the Grand Hotel, but it was full – so they stayed with us instead.*

Practice

The first column describes what Jan planned to do: the second describes what actually happened. In your notebook, write how he describes his life, using one sentence for each number. Add the conjunctions **and**, **so**, **but**, where necessary.

Plan
1 Go to university.

2 Find a job in Madrid.

3 Study English in London.

4 Stay with an English family.

5 Study English for two years.

6 Work in England when I finish school.

7 Not going to work in my parents' restaurant.

Reality
1 Failed exams. Left school at sixteen.

2 No jobs. Decided to go to England to study English.

3 Didn't like London. Went to Cambridge instead.

4 Changed my mind. Stayed in a student hostel.

5 Didn't have enough money. Finished after eighteen months.

6 Couldn't find a job. Came back to Madrid.

7 Needed the money. I did.

Example: 1 *I was going to go to university, but I failed my*
          exams, so I left school at sixteen.

SIMPLE, CONTINUOUS AND PERFECT ASPECTS

26 Tenses

Check

Copy this table into your notebook and give an example of the positive, question, and negative of each tense.

	Tense	Verb	Positive	Question	Negative
1	Present Simple	she/agree	She agrees	Does she agree?	She doesn't agree
2	Present Continuous	he/leave	He's leaving		
3	Past Simple	they/leave			
4	Past Continuous	he/shout			
5	Present Perfect Simple	they/arrive			
6	Present Perfect Continuous	she/work			
7	Past Perfect Simple	they/go			
8	Past Perfect Continuous	they/sleep			
9	Future Simple	he/leave			
10	Future Continuous	they/work/ tomorrow			
11	Future Perfect Simple	they/leave/ by tomorrow			
12	Future Perfect Continuous	they/work/ all day			

27 Simple and continuous aspects

The **tense** of a verb tells us that it is present, past, or future; the **aspect** gives us other information. There are three aspects – simple, continuous, and perfect.
The simple aspect refers to the whole of an activity or event, and not just part of it:
I'll have a bath tonight. (future simple)
I worked from eight o'clock to ten o'clock. (past simple)
I go to the office by car. (present simple)

It is used to describe:

- a general truth:
  Big cars use a lot of petrol.

- a repeated, habitual action:
  Classes start at nine o'clock.

- a complete event or series of events:
  We went to Spain for our holiday.

- feelings, perceptions, etc. – i.e. any verb that is not an 'activity' verb:
  I understood the lecture quite well.

The continuous aspect describes an event (or series of events) at some point between its beginning and its end. It is used with activity verbs – e.g. **play**, **run**, **walk**, **go**, **move**, **drive**, etc. – and it is the activity which is important, rather than the end result:

They're working at the moment. (present continuous)
I was reading when you phoned. (past continuous)
At this time tomorrow we'll be saying goodbye. (future continuous)

It is used to describe:

* an activity in progress:
  I was working in the garden when she called.

* a repeated action which is temporary, and viewed at some time between the beginning and end of the temporary period:
  I'm cycling to work this week because my car's in the garage.

* a temporary situation viewed at some point between its beginning and its end:
  I'm living in London at the moment.

Practice

Choose between the simple and continuous aspects in the following sentences. If two answers are possible, write them both. Do this exercise in your notebook:

1   'Where's Stella?'
    'She (play) tennis in the park.' (present)
    'She's playing tennis in the park.'
2   They (go) abroad three times last year. (past)
3   I (see) you outside the cinema at eight o'clock. (future)
4   The telephone (ring) but I (watch) my favourite programme so I (not answer) it. (past)
5   Simon (work) really hard for his exams next month. (present)
6   He (live) away from home when he starts college. (future)
7   Cats (not like) water. (present)
8   I (not understand) what she (mean) at first, but then she (explain) more clearly. (past)
9   I think I (make) a cup of tea. (future)
10 The bottle (roll) off the table and (smash) when it (hit) the floor. (past)
11 I (call) at the office but they (all work) so I (not stay) long. (past)
12 I (see) my parents tonight so I (give) them your message then. (future)
13 I (not understand) a single word he (say). (present)
14 Five or six people (wait) to see Mrs Blackstone. (present)
15 The bottle (roll) off the table, but I (catch) it before it (go) over the edge. (past)

28 Perfect aspect

The perfect aspect can be either simple or continuous. It tells us:

- that the activity or state being discussed occurs or starts before a certain point in time: and
- that the activity or state has an important connection with that later point in time:

  I *have been* to France twice. (present perfect: the events occurred before the present time – now)

  It was 1946. The war *had finished* and Jack *had left* the army. (past perfect: the events occurred before the past time – 1946)

  Come tomorrow at 7.30. I'*ll have had* dinner by then. (future perfect: dinner will occur before a future time – tomorrow at 7.30)

Practice

In your notebook, write the sentences below, putting the verbs into the present perfect, past perfect or future perfect, and using the simple or continuous forms.

1 (You see) that film yet?
   Have you seen that film yet?
2 I (write) letters all day, and I'm tired.
   I've been writing letters all day, and I'm tired.
3 I (not play) football since I was at school.
4 How long (you wait) to see the doctor?
5 They (talk) but they stopped when I came into the room.
6 By the end of this month, I (work) here for ten years.
7 When I arrived, the party (finish).
8 We've got two more hours. We (do) all the housework by the time your parents arrive.
9 I (read) that book for two months but I (not finish) it yet.
10 They (wait) for me for two hours when I finally arrived.
11 We (know) each other since we were at school together.
12 They (try) to solve the problem for some time now.
13 The machines (work) continuously for two years when they get their first service next month.
14 We (work) on the car for two hours before it finally started.
15 By tomorrow, they (get) permission to have the meeting at the town hall, I'm sure.
16 (anyone arrive) when you got to the office?
17 She looks very tired – I think she (do) too much overtime.
18 I (not see) her for the last five years.
19 (You say) goodnight to the children yet?
20 When I got there, I could see that they (not expect) me.

VERB FORMATIONS

29 Irregular verbs

Practice

29a Write the missing words for these irregular verbs.

Infinitive	Past Simple	Past Participle	Infinitive	Past Simple	Past Participle
bet	bet	bet	rise	rose	risen
bite	bit	bitten	sew	sewed	sewn
bleed	bled	bled	shake	shook	shaken
creep	crept	crept	shrink	shrank	shrunk
dig	dug	dug	sink	sank	sunk
feed	fed	fed	slide	slid	slid
flee	fled	fled	spit	spat	spat
freeze	froze	frozen	split	split	split
hang	hung	hung	spread	spread	spread
lay	laid	laid	stick	stuck	stuck
lead	led	led	swing	swung	swung
leap	leapt	leapt	tear	tore	torn
mistake	mistook	mistaken	wake	woke	woken
ring	rang	rung	weep	wept	wept

29b Complete these sentences, choosing the most appropriate verb from the table and putting it into the present perfect or past simple.

1 Ow! Your dog *has bitten* me on the leg!

2 After stealing the money, the thieves *split* it between them.

3 Look! Those workmen ..... *dug* .... another big hole in the road.

4 Inflation . *has risen* .... by 2% this year.

5 After the invasion, thousands of refugees ..... *fled* .... to other countries.

6 ...... *Have* .... they ...... *rung* .... the bell yet?

7 You sound very sleepy. .... *have* .... you just ..... *woken* .... up?

8 The ship ..... *sank* .... after it hit an iceberg.

9 Your sweater . *has shrunk* . You should take it back to the shop and complain.

10 As soon as it was light, our guide ..... *led* .... us through the forest.

37

30 Verbs taking gerund, infinitive, or indirect speech

- Some verbs are followed
  by the infinitive:
  She advised me **to go**.

- Some verbs use the gerund:
  I like **driving**.

- Some verbs use indirect speech:
  They complained **that they had
  been waiting for hours**.

- Certain verbs can use all three.
  We agreed **to go**.
  We agreed **that we should go**.
  We agreed **about going**.

Note: Exercise 30c combines the answers from 30a and 30b in a table. Both exercises show
constructions commonly following the verbs given; sometimes the verb is followed by
more than one construction. Phrasal verbs (e.g. **ask after**, **finish off**, etc.) are not
included, neither are less common constructions or prepositions.

Practice

30a Make sentences using the constructions given. Put the verbs into the past
simple tense.

1. (accuse of + gerund)

   They .... me / take the money.

   They accused me of taking the money.

2. (advise + to-infinitive)

   She .... me / wait.

   She advised me to wait.

   (advise + gerund)

   She .... wait / for a while.

   She advised waiting for a while.

   (advise + that-indirect speech)

   She .... / they / wait.

   She advised that they should wait.

3. (agree + to-infinitive; agree on / about + gerund; agree + that-indirect
   speech)

   We .... / leave early.

   We agreed to leave early.

   We agreed on/about leaving early.

   We agreed that we should leave early.

4   (apologize for + gerund)

I .... / be late.

I apologized for being late.

5   (as + to-infinitive; ask + if-indirect speech)

Peter .... / speak to Janice.

Peter asked to speak to Janice.

Peter asked if he could speak to Janice.

6   (begin + to-infinitive; begin + gerund)

We .... / read the instructions.

7   (believe in + gerund; believe + that-indirect speech)

We .... / tell the truth.

8   (complain about + gerund; complain + that-indirect speech)

They .... / be hungry.

9   (continue + to-infinitive; continue + gerund)

Mary .... / work at home.

10 (decide + to-infinitive; decide + that-indirect speech; decide on + gerund)

We all .... / have a picnic.

11 (dream + that-indirect speech; dream of/about + gerund)

I .... / fly to the moon.

12 (encourage + to-infinitive)

They .... / me / practise every day.

13 (enjoy + gerund)

He .... / swim a lot.

14 (expect + to-infinitive; expect + that-indirect speech)

She .... / go to Paris for the summer.

15 (finish + gerund)

They .... / eat at ten.

16 (forget + to-infinitive; forget about + gerund; forget + that-indirect speech)

I .... / phone my mother.

17 (hate + gerund; hate + to-infinitive)

She .... / be bored.

30b Decide if the following sentences can be finished correctly by A, B, and/or C. Sometimes all three are possible.

1 (help) We all helped

   Ⓐ to move the car. B moving the car. C that the car moved.

2 (hope) I had hoped

   Ⓐ to be able to come soon. B for coming soon.

   Ⓒ that I'd be able to come soon.

3 (insist) They insist

   A to see the manager. B on seeing the manager.

   C that they should see the manager.

4 (intend) I intend

   A stay here for some time. B staying here for some time.

   C that I should stay here for some time.

5 (invite) We invited them

   A to come to the party. B for coming to the party.

   C that they should come to the party.

6 (know) They already knew

   A to leave. B about leaving early. C that they should leave early.

7 (learn) John soon learned

   A to work the machine. B about working the machine.

   C that he should work the machine.

8 (let) Why didn't they let

   A him go? B him going? C that he should go?

9 (love) the children love

   A to play with Mark. B playing with Mark.

   C that they should play with Mark.

10 (make) They made

   A him stay. B him staying. C that he should stay.

11 (manage) We finally managed

   A to open the car door. B opening the car door.

   C that we opened the car door.

12 (mind) Do you mind

   A me to smoke? B my smoking? C if I smoke?

13 (miss) I miss

   A to live near my family. B living near my family.

   C that I don't live near my family.

14 (offer) They offered

   A to pay for the damage. B paying for the damage.

   C that they would pay for the damage.

15 (order) He ordered
   A them to stay there. B them staying there.
   C that they should stay there.

16 (plan) We planned
   A to arrive at nine o'clock. B on arriving at nine o'clock.
   C that we should arrive at nine o'clock.

17 (prefer) I prefer
   A to work alone. B working alone. C that I should work alone.

18 (promise) They promised
   A to visit her. B about visiting her. C that they would visit her.

19 (recommend) I would recommend
   A you to have the seafood. B having the seafood.
   C that you have the seafood.

20 (refuse) They refused
   A to leave. B leaving. C that they would leave.

21 (remember) I remembered
   A to pick up my keys. B picking up my keys
   C that I had picked up my keys.

22 (seem) You seem
   A to be tired. B being tired. C that you are tired.

23 (start) After an hour, we started
   A to work more slowly. B working more slowly.
   C that we worked more slowly.

24 (stop) Some time later, they stopped
   A to rest. B working. C that they should rest.

25 (suggest) She suggested
   A to go to a different school. B going to a different school.
   C that we should go to a different school.

26 (think) I thought
   A to go abroad. B of/about going abroad. C that I would go abroad.

27 (tell) They told me
   A to leave early. B about leaving early. C that I should leave early.

28 (try) Please try
   A to speak more quietly. B speaking more quietly.
   C that you should speak more quietly.

29 (want) Do you want
   A to go home? B going home? C that you should go home?

30 (warn) I warned him
   A to be careful. B against driving too fast.
   C that he shouldn't drive too fast.

30c Fill in the following table according to the answers you have given in exercises 30a and 30b. If the gerund is preceded by a particular preposition, write the preposition in the box.

	Infinitive	Gerund	Indirect Speech		Infinitive	Gerund	Indirect Speech
accuse		✓ of		let			
advise	✓	✓	✓	love			
agree	✓	✓ on about	✓	make			
apologize		✓ for		manage			
ask				mind			
begin				miss			
believe				offer			
complain				order			
continue				plan			
decide				prefer			
dream				promise			
encourage				recommend			
enjoy				refuse			
expect				remember			
finish				seem			
forget				start			
hate				stop			
help				suggest			
hope				think			
insist				tell			
intend				try			
invite				want			
know				warn			
learn							

Note: *seem* can be followed by *that* when used with *it*:
It seems that they aren't coming.

THE PASSIVE

31   The passive: Present Simple, Past Simple, Present Perfect Simple

- Passive sentences describe what happens to people or things, often as a result of action by other people or things.

- Passive sentences often indicate that what happens is more important than who is responsible. For example:

Active
Simon has painted the house.
The speaker is talking about Simon and the house.

Passive
The house has been painted.
Only the house is being discussed and not the person who painted it.

FORM

Present	noun/pronoun + **is/are**	+ past participle
	The cars are	taken abroad.
Past	noun/pronoun + **was/were**	+ past participle
	The cars were	taken abroad.
Present Perfect	noun/pronoun + **has/have been**	+ past participle
	The cars have been	taken abroad.

- The rules for choice of tense are the same in the passive as they are for active sentences.

➤ Exercise 32 for passives in all tenses.

Practice

Rewrite these sentences, putting the verbs in the passive. Keep them in the same tense, and remove *they, we, someone*, etc.

1   We clean the garages every day.

   The garages are cleaned every day.

2   Someone has given him a lot of money.

   He has been given a lot of money.   le han dado mucho dinero

3   The police arrested two hundred people.

   Two hundred people were arrested.

4   We check every car engine thoroughly.   completo (arriba abajo)

   Every car engine thoroughly is checked.

5   We export this computer to seventy different countries.

   this computer is exported to seventy different countries

6 They have cancelled the meeting.

the meeting have been cancelled

7 We opened the factory at nine o'clock.

the factory was opened at nine o'clock

8 They send two million books to America every year.

Two million books are sent to America every year

9 We have invited all the students in the school.

All the students in the school have been invited

10 We have told him not to be late again.

He has been told not to be late again

11 They posted all the letters yesterday.

All the letters were posted yesterday

12 The machine wraps the bread automatically.

the bread is wrapped automatically

13 They paid me a lot of money to do the job.

I was paid a lot of money to do the job

14 Fortunately, they didn't damage the machinery.

Fortunately, the machinery wasn't damaged

15 We send the newspapers to Scotland by train.

The newspapers are sent to Scotland by train.

32 The passive: all tenses, simple and continuous

FORM

Present	Simple:	**is/are** + *past participle*
		The letters are delivered here.
	Continuous:	**is/are being** + *past participle*
		He's being interviewed at the moment.

Past	Simple:	**was/were** + *past participle*
		They were sent by train.
	Continuous:	**is/were being** + *past participle*
		My suit was being cleaned at the time.

Present Perfect	*Simple:*	**has/have been** + *past participle*
		All the tickets have been sold.
	Continuous: –	

Past Perfect	*Simple:*	**had been** + *past participle*
		I was too late: the papers had been removed.
	Continuous: –	

Future	*Simple:*	**will be** + *past participle*
		You will be met at the station.
	Continuous: –	

Infinitive	**(to) be** + *past participle*	*Gerund*	He doesn't like
	I don't want to be arrested.		be**ing** told
	We shouldn't be arrested.		what to do.

Notes

- The passive is frequently used to describe scientific or mechanical processes, or in formal explanations:
  *The passive **is** frequently **used** ...*

- It is not essential to repeat the auxiliary verb ***to be*** in a list of processes:
  The cars are washed, cleaned, checked, and then driven to the ports.

Practice

32a Underline all the passives.

Acid rain <u>is caused</u> by burning coal or oil. When either fuel <u>is burned</u>, it releases poisonous gases which <u>are carried</u> up into the atmosphere and sometimes <u>transported</u> long distances.

Over 3,000 research projects have been carried out to look into acid rain, and a decision to tackle the problem has been taken in most of the western European countries. Measures have been taken in Scandinavia and in Central Europe to stop the pollution before it is dumped on the environment, and a diplomatic campaign has been launched to convince other countries that the problem has to be considered as a major ecological threat.

'Five years ago this issue was not being treated seriously,' says one leading environmental group, 'but now that damage has been reported in large areas of forest and lakeland, our politicians are being forced to take action. This problem must be solved quickly: if governments do nothing, they will be faced in two or three years' time with the accusation that they have allowed our forests to die.' A major international initiative to combat acid rain is expected in the near future.

32b Rewrite these sentences in the passive. The subject of the active sentence can usually be omitted; you should include it in the passive sentence only if it is necessary.

1 Someone's interviewing Dr Johnson at the moment.

Dr Johnson *'s being interviewed at the moment.*

2 You mustn't use this machine after 5.30 p.m.

This machine *mustn't be used after 5.30 p.m.*

3 We had warned him the day before not to go too near the canal.

He *had been warned the day before not go too near the canal*

4 They were painting the outside of the ship when the accident happened.

The outside of the ship *was being painted when the accident happened.*

5 You must clean this machine every time you use it.

This machine *must be cleaned every time you use it.*

6 You should keep the flowers in a warm sunny place.

The flowers *should be kept in a warm sunny place.*

7 They're mending your shoes at the moment.

Your shoes *are being mended at the moment.*

8 Someone will drive your car to Edinburgh on Tuesday.

Your car *will be driven to Edinburgh on Tuesday.*

9 We don't allow smoking in this restaurant.

Smoking *isn't allowed in this restaurant.*

10 You should pay your bill before you leave the hotel.

Your bill *should be paid before you leave the hotel.*

11 I have told the children about the party.

The children *have been told about the party.*

12 About thirty million people are watching this programme.

This programme *is being watched about thirty million people.*

13 We expect students not to talk during the examination.

Students *are expected not to talk during the examination.*

14 You mustn't touch this button while the experiment is in progress.
This button *mustn't be touched while the experiment is in progress.*

15 Someone will blow a whistle if there is an emergency.
A whistle *will be blown if there is an emergency.*

16 Someone was carrying the bomb to a safe place when it exploded.
The bomb *was being carried to a safe place when it exploded.*

17 Someone's moved my chair!
My chair *was moved.*

18 The police are questioning Mr and Mrs Davidson.
Mr and Mrs Davidson *are being questioned by the police.*

19 Someone checks the water level every week.
The water level *is checked every week.*

20 We invited two hundred people to the wedding.
Two hundred people *were invited to the wedding.*

33 *to have something done*

FORM

> *subject* + **has/have** + *object* + *past participle*
> James   has   his car   cleaned every week.

USE

- To describe an action which I (or you, he, she, etc.) arrange but do not do myself:
  I had my suit cleaned last week.
  She's going to have her house repaired by the Council.

Notes

- All tenses are possible:
  I'm having my house painted at the moment. (present continuous)
  I've had the car fixed. (present perfect)
  I'll have your coat cleaned for you. (future)

- Note the word order. The object goes before the past participle – there is a difference between:
  He had his car cleaned. and *He had cleaned his car.*
- *Get* can be used in the same way as *have*:
  She's going to get her house repaired by the Council.
- Note the colloquial use:
  I had my bag stolen last week.
  This is not an arranged action.

Practice

In your notebook, rewrite these sentences using *have* + object + past participle and changing some words if necessary.

1　Someone delivers the newspapers. (We)
　We have the newspapers delivered.
2　Someone cleaned the carpets every year. (I)
　I had the carpets cleaned every year.
3　Their house needs painting. (They're going to)
　They're going to have their house painted.
4　We ask someone to check the accounts every month. (We)
5　Someone sends the money to my bank account in London. (I)
6　My stereo isn't working properly. It needs cleaning. (I'm going to)
7　My camera's being repaired at the moment. (I'm)
8　He spilt coffee on my jacket so he took it away for cleaning. (He spilt coffee on my jacket so he)
9　I think it's time to service the car. (It's time to)
10　I don't like the office curtains. It's time to change them. (I think I'll)
11　There's something wrong with the typewriter. It needs repairing. (I think I'll)
12　We couldn't go to Jack's flat: it was being painted. (We couldn't go to Jack's flat: he)
13　The computer's no good: we're changing it. (We)
14　I send the films to England: they are processed there. (I)
15　I didn't want to eat in the hotel dining-room, so I asked them to send a meal up to my room. (I didn't want to eat in the hotel dining-room, so I)

MISCELLANEOUS

34　*wish*

- *wish* can be followed by several different tenses: *wish* + past simple, *wish* + past perfect, and *wish* + *would* + infinitive.

a) *wish* + past simple

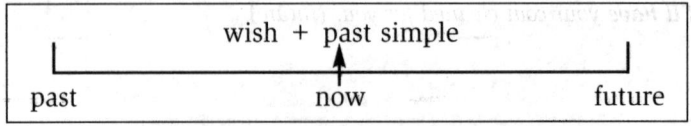

I wish things were different now.

This expresses an unrealistic desire for the present situation to be different. The desire is unrealistic because there is very little chance of the change occurring.

I wish I was rich.

FORM

subject + **wish** + *past simple*		
I	wish	I was rich.
I	wish	I lived in America.
Do you	wish	we lived nearer the school?

Note: This past simple can have a special form with the verb *to be*: *were* instead of *was* (in formal or written English). So we can say:

*I wish I **were** rich.* or *I wish I **was** rich.*
*He wishes he **were** rich.* or *He wishes he **was** rich.*

Practice

34a Rewrite these sentences using *I wish* + past simple.

1 I'd love to live in Australia.

   I wish I lived in Australia.

2 I hate having to go to school on Saturdays.

   I wish I didn't have to go to school on Saturdays.

3 Why don't we go away more often?

   ....

4 I'd love to be a film star.

   ....

5 Why don't we have a bigger house?

   ....

6 I'd love to speak more languages.

   ....

7 I'd love to be able to cook.

   ....

8 Why is the school so expensive?

   ....

9 I never have enough money: it would be nice to have more.

   ....

10 I hate having to do homework every night.

   ....

b) **wish** + past perfect

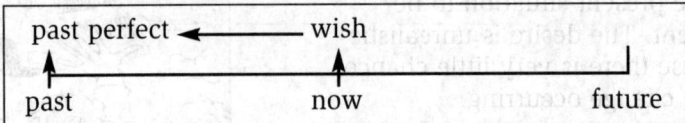

I wish things had been different in the past.

This expresses a desire that an action or event in the past had been different.

FORM

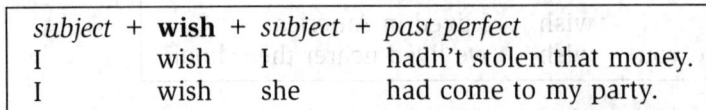

subject + **wish** + *subject* + *past perfect*
I   wish   I   hadn't stolen that money.
I   wish   she   had come to my party.

Practice

34b Rewrite these sentences using *I wish* + past perfect.

1   I decided to work in London.

   I wish I hadn't decided to work in London.

2   We didn't go to Alan's party.

   I wish we'd gone to Alan's party.

3   We went to live with my parents in Surrey.

   ....

4   I decided to stop working as a bus driver.

   ....

5   We put our money into a grocery shop.

   ....

6   We borrowed £3,000 to start the business.

   ....

7   We didn't realise that a supermarket was opening nearby.

   ....

8   The grocery shop closed down.

   ....

9   We lost all our money.

   ....

10 It was a mistake to leave Manchester.

   ....

c) *wish* + *would* + infinitive

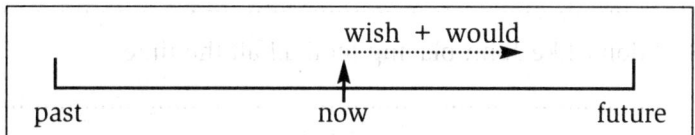

I wish things would change soon.

This expresses annoyance with a person or situation and a desire for a situation to change, either now or in the future. The change could possibly occur, but we do not expect it to. It generally depends on action from some other person or thing.

FORM

subject +	**wish** +	subject +	**would** +	infinitive
I	wish	he	would	give up smoking.
I	wish	it	would	stop raining.
I	wish	she	would	be more careful.

- *would* can be shortened to *'d*:
  I wish she'd be more careful.
- Note the difference between this and
  the *'d* (= *had*) in the *past perfect*:
  I wish she'd been more careful.

*I wish it would
stop raining.*

Practice

34c Mr and Mrs Reynolds are worried about their children. Write what they want them to do, using *I wish* + *would*.

1 John never comes home before twelve o'clock.

   I wish John would come home before twelve o'clock.

2 Sheila isn't very polite to her grandparents.

   I wish Sheila would be more polite to her grandparents.

3 Peter doesn't wash very often.

   ....

4 Susan isn't working very hard for her exams.

   ....

5 John doesn't help with the housework.

   ....

6 I'd like Peter to give up smoking.

   ....

7   Sheila takes too many days off work.

....

8   I don't like John playing football all the time.

....

9   Sheila and Susan are very unkind to Peter.

....

10 John doesn't wear a tie very often.

....

Note: *if only* can be used instead of **wish** in all three constructions described above. It is stronger and more unrealistic than **wish**:
If only I was rich.
If only I hadn't stolen that money.
If only it would stop raining.

35   *wish*

Check

35a Answer 'Yes' or 'No' and circle (i) or (ii).

1 I wish I had a big car.
   a) Do I have a big car? ...*No*...
   b) Am I talking about (i) the present?
                         (ii) the past?

2 I wish I'd gone to university.
   a) Did I go to university? ....
   b) Am I talking about (i) the present?
                         (ii) the past?

3 If only she'd take the new job.
   a) Has she agreed to take the new job? ....
   b) Am I talking about (i) the past?
                         (ii) the present/future?

4 I wish they hadn't phoned the police.
   a) Did they phone the police? ....
   b) Am I talking about (i) the past?
                         (ii) the present/future?

5 I wish she spoke French.
   a) Can she speak French? ....
   b) Did she speak French? ....
   c) Are we talking about (i) the past?
                          (ii) the present?

6 I wish she would speak French.

   a) Can she speak French? ....

   b) Is she speaking French? ....

   c) Are we talking about (i) the past?

                                (ii) the present/future?

7 I wish I could agree with you.

   a) Do I agree with you? ....

   b) Am I going to change my mind? ....

   c) Am I talking about (i) the past?

                                (ii) the present?

8 If only he'd agreed with us.

   a) Did he agree with us? ....

   b) Am I talking about (i) the present?

                                (ii) the past?

35b Circle the correct verb form in each sentence.

1 I wish it (*stopped* / *would stop*) raining.

2 I wish it (*hadn't snowed* / *wouldn't snow*) yesterday.

3 I wish (*I knew* / *I'd know*) the answer to your question.

4 I wish you (*wouldn't be* / *aren't*) so rude.

5 I wish (*they visited* / *they'd visited*) us when they were in town.

6 I wish (*I'd speak* / *I spoke*) better French.

7 I wish they (*hadn't been* / *wouldn't have been*) so unfriendly.

8 I wish (*I've refused* / *I'd refused*) when you suggested the idea.

9 I wish (*I had* / *would have*) more time to do this job.

10 I wish she (*would* / *had*) come to work on time in future.

Conditionals

36 First, second and zero conditionals

> **REMEMBER!**

First conditional

FORM

if + present simple	*future*
If it's hot tomorrow,	*we'll go to the beach.*
or	
future	*if* + present simple
We'll go to the beach	*if it's hot.*

USE

• To talk about what will happen in the future when there is a possibility that the event in the *if*-clause might happen.

Second conditional

FORM

if + *was*/*were*/past simple	*would*/*could*/*might* + infinitive
If I was rich	*I could buy a yacht.*
If Peter got that job	*we'd move to Edinburgh.*
or	
would/*could*/*might* + infinitive	*if* + *was*/*were*/past simple
I could buy a yacht	*if I was rich.*
We'd move to Edinburgh	*if Peter got that job.*

USE

• To talk about the present when the event in the *if*-clause is not true:
  I could buy a yacht if I was rich. (I'm not rich.)

• To talk about the future when the event in the *if*-clause is unlikely to happen:
  We'd move to Edinburgh if Peter got that job. (I don't think he will get the job.)

Zero conditional

FORM

if + present simple	present simple
If I go to bed late,	*I always feel tired the next day.*
If you cook vegetables for too long,	*they taste awful.*
or	
present simple	*if* + present simple
I always feel tired the next day	*if I go to bed late.*
Vegetables taste awful	*if you cook them for too long.*

USE

• To talk about things that always/often/sometimes happen if something else (in the *if*-clause) happens.

Practice

Write these sentences, putting the verbs in brackets into the correct form and adding 'll/will, or 'd/would if necessary.

1 If you give me your phone number, I (call) *'ll call* you.

2 I (drive) *'d drive* to work if I had a car.

3 If I (lose) *lost* my job, I'd go back to university.

4 If it (rain) *rains* tomorrow, we'll cancel the barbecue.

5 Where would you live if you (can) *could* choose?

6 If the weather (be) *is* good, we often have lunch outside.

7 My mother (worry) *would worry* about me if I didn't phone her every week.

8 If you finish before 5 o'clock, I (come) *'ll come* and pick you up.

9 If we (hurry) *hurried*, we'll get to the shops before they close.

10 I don't know what she (do) *would do* if she couldn't go on working.

11 What would you do if he (ask) *asked* you to marry him?

12 He always (complain) *complains* if I'm late.

13 If I knew the answer to that question, I (tell) *would tell* you.

14 If you come to the party, you (meet) *will meet* Jim.

15 The students usually work hard if they (have) *have* a test.

16 Where will you wait if I (be) *am* delayed?

17 If she (speak) *spoke* more clearly, I could understand her.

18 If you (win) *won* a lot of money, what would you do with it?

19 If the club (close) *closed*, where would we go?

20 I'll see him at the meeting if he (come) *comes* .

37 The third conditional

FORM

> *if* + *past perfect*   *would/could/might* + *perfect infinitive*
> If I had met you earlier, I wouldn't have married Joe.
> If I'd worked harder, I would have passed the exam.
>
> or *would/could/might* + *perfect infinitive*   *if* + *past perfect*
> I wouldn't have married Jo if I'd met you earlier.
> I would have passed the exam if I'd worked harder.

USE

- The third conditional refers to the past (it is sometimes called the past conditional):

  I'd have warned you if I'd seen you last week. (but I didn't see you, so I didn't warn you)

  If I'd passed by exams, I would have gone to Art College. (but I didn't pass my exams, so I didn't go to Art College)

Practice

Write these sentences in full, using the words given. Put the verbs into the correct tense.

1 What / would / you / done / if / I not / lend / you / the money?

   What would you have done if I hadn't lent you the money?

2 If / you / asked / me for tickets / I / could / get / you some.

   If you had asked me for tickets, I could have got you some.

3 I / not / marry / him / if / I / know / what he was like.

   I wouldn't ~~have~~ marry him if I had known what he was like.

4 I / not / hire / a car / if / I / know / how expensive it was.

   I wouldn't ~~have~~ hire a car if I had known expensive it was

5 If / we / got / to the cinema earlier / we / not / miss / the start of the film.

   If we had got to the cinema earlier we wouldn't ~~had~~ missed the start of the film.

6 If / I / be born / a year earlier / I / have to do / military service.

   If I had been born a year earlier I would have ~~had~~ to do military service.

7 If / you / asked / me / I / would lend / you my car.

If you had asked me I would have lend you my car.

8 If / I gone / to university / I / get / a better job.

If I had gone to university I would had got a better job

9 I / wouldn't / go out / yesterday / if / you asked / me not to.

I wouldn't have go out yesterday if you had asked me not to

10 I / could / give you / a lift / if / my car / not broken down.

I could have given you a lift if my car hadn't broken down

11 I / not go / to Berlin / if / I know / what was going to happen.

I wouldn't have go to Berlin if I had known what was going to happen

12 I would / stay / longer / if / she / wanted me to .

I would have stayed longer if she had wanted me to.

13 I / not come / to this school / if / I / know / what it was like.

I wouldn't have come to this school if I had known what it was like

14 We / would go / to his party / if / we / able to / find a baby-sitter.

We would have gone to his party if we had been able to find a baby-sitter

15 I / visit / you / in hospital / if / I / know / you were there.

I would have visited you in hospital if I had known you were there

38 Words other than *if*

- Other words can be used instead of *if* in conditional clauses:
  a) **unless** = 'if not':
  I'll go home soon if the film doesn't start.
  I'll go home soon unless the film starts.

  b) **provided (that), on condition (that), <u>as long as</u>, so long as**:
  Provided that everybody agrees, we'll have the meeting on Tuesday.

  c) **(just) suppose, supposing (that), what if, imagine**:
  Just suppose it didn't rain for four months: would we have enough water?

The words are not always interchangeable. Their use depends on the context of the sentence.

Practice

Underline the correct word or words to replace the words in italics in these sentences.

1 'I'll give you £100 *if* you say nothing about this.' (<u>provided that</u>, what if, unless)

2 '*If* your company went bankrupt, what would you do?' (just suppose, on condition, as long as)

3 '*If* you had to live in another country, where would you go?' (on condition, unless, imagine)

4 'We'll let him out of prison *if* he reports to the police station every day. (supposing, as long as, unless)

5 'I'll take them to court *if* they *don't* pay me what they owe.' (imagine, provided that, unless)

6 '*If* you won a million pounds – what would you do with it?' (providing, as long as, unless, imagine)

7 '*If* they keep to the agreement, I'll give them the money.' (what if, imagine, so long as)

8 'You'll be alright *if* you take some travellers' cheques.' (provided that, imagine, what if)

9 'I'll complain to the manager *if* you *don't* give me a different room.' (as long as, unless, imagine)

10 '*If* all the hotels were full, were would we stay?' (provided that, as long as, suppose)

39　Sentences containing hidden conditions

- Conditional sentences are sometimes long and complicated, and they are not always fully expressed in conversation – especially where *if*-event has already been mentioned, or can be understood from the context of the conversation:
  'James didn't come to the party.'
  'What a pity. I'm sure he would have enjoyed it.'

  The second statement depends on the hidden condition 'if he had come':
  I'm sure he would have enjoyed it (if he had come).

- Other examples of hidden conditions:
  'Be careful, Tom. I wouldn't hurry this decision.' (if I were you)
  You should have come. You would have loved it.' (if you had come)

Practice

Underline the clauses containing hidden conditions.

1

MR ANDERSON:　I don't think he should go.

MRS ANDERSON:　Why not? He's sixteen, he's old enough. I'm sure <u>he wouldn't do anything stupid</u>.

MR ANDERSON:　You know him – he'd get involved in a fight. I don't think he could look after himself. He'd get hurt!

MRS ANDERSON:　I'm sure he'd keep out of trouble.

MR ANDERSON:　Are you? Well, I'm not. I don't think we should let him go.

2

MARTHA:　I think we should go to Scotland for the holiday. I'm fed up with going abroad and getting sick. We'd enjoy ourselves more in Scotland.

JAMES:　Oh, I don't think so. The weather's terrible up there. We wouldn't be able to sunbathe or go swimming. There'd be nothing to do.

MARTHA:　We could go walking in the mountains. That would be lovely.

JAMES:　Well, I think it would be dangerous. You know what terrible mists they have in Scotland. There are always stories about people getting lost in the mountains.

MARTHA:　How about going with a group – the Youth Club, for instance?

JAMES:　Oh, you know you'd hate that. You can't stand organized holidays ...

40 Mixed tense conditionals

Although conditionals are usually presented as first, second or third conditionals
(➤ Exercises 36 and 37), the present simple does not always have to go with the
future simple, *would* does not always have to go with the past simple, etc.:
If I'd stayed at school, I would be in university now. (past event with
consequences in the present)
If you hear the alarm, get out as fast as you can. (general condition +
imperative)
I'll take your plate if you've finished. (future simple often dependent on present
perfect event)
If he saw us, he always said hello. (zero conditional in past tense)

Practice

Match the two halves of the sentences.

1 If he was happy, ...*E*....

2 If you hadn't lost your job ....,

3 If she didn't lose her temper so quickly, ...

4 If she doesn't do her work, ...

5 Can I borrow your pen, ...

6 If the machine stopped, ...

7 You wouldn't be so hungry ....

8 Whistle ....

9 If I study here for another month, ...

10 If it's raining. ....

A we stopped.

B she wouldn't have got into that fight.

C I wouldn't go out for a walk.

D I'll have been here for a year.

E I was happy.

F send her home.

G if you'd eaten a proper breakfast.

H we wouldn't be living here.

I if you see the police coming.

J if you've finished using it?

41 The conditionals

Check

Write these sentences, putting the verbs into the correct tense.

1 If you'd stayed at home, there (not be) _wouldn't have been_ any trouble.

2 What would you do if he (resign) _resigned_ tomorrow?

3 It's a pity John didn't come to the football. He (liked) _would have liked_ it.

4 I'll do it if he (ask) ...asks... me.

5 I wouldn't have been so upset if Judy (write) ...had written... to me earlier.

6 If we offered him more money, (he stay) ...would he stay... here?

7 If she's gone out, we (ask) ...will ask... Peter to do it for us.

8 I (look after) ...will look after... the bags if you carry the children.

9 We would have missed the train if we (be) ...had been... two minutes later.

10 It's a pity Terry wasn't at the party. He (love) ...would have loved... it.

11 Phone the police if you (see) ...will see... anything strange.

12 I'm going to scream if you (not stop) ...don't stop... playing that guitar.

13 The children always (get) ...get... frightened if they watch horror films.

14 (You let me know) ...Will you let me know... what happens if I don't get to the meeting?

15 I don't know what I'd do if John (be) ...was... in an accident.

16 There (be) ...will be... trouble if they try to stop him leaving.

17 Can I take the typewriter if you (finish) ...*will finish*...... with it?

18 It's a pity David isn't here. He (be) ...*would be*........ very
amused. → *entretenido*.

19 Shout if you (see) ....*see*.......... anything unusual.

20 If you (look after) .....*look after*.... the car, it will never break
down.

21 If you (look after) ...*looked after*.... the car, it wouldn't break
down so much.

22 If you (look after) .*had looked after*. the car, we'd be able to sell
it now.

23 Why didn't you watch that programme? You (enjoy) *would enjoyed* *haven't*
.... it.

24 If he weren't so bad-tempered, his wife (not leave) ...*haven't left*... *would*
.... him so soon after the marriage.

25 (Ask) ....*Ask*......... for help if you're having problems.

26 I (not go out) ...*have gone out*... if I'd known he was so ill. *wouldn't*

27 What (you say) *would you say*... if I offered you a job?

28 He (be) ....*will be*.. tired when we see him tomorrow if
he's been working all night.

29 Tell me if there (be) ....*is*.............. anything wrong.

30 The engine starts if you (turn) ...*turn*.................. this key.

➤ Exercise 54 for a comparison of **could**, **would**, and **might**.

Modals

'Modals' are the small verbs like **can**, **must**, and **might**, which give certain meanings to main verbs.

There are twelve modal verbs:
**can, could, shall, should, must, ought to,
may, might, will, would, need (to), dare**

son iguales: debería
atreverse a hacer algo
o osar

FORM

- Positive is formed by putting the modal between the subject and the main verb.
  We should stay.

- Negative is formed by adding **not** (or **n't**) after the modal:
  We shouldn't stay.

- Questions are formed by changing the position of the modal and the subject:
  Should we stay? Shouldn't we stay?

Notes

- **need** can be **needn't** (modal form) or **don't need to** (verb form).

- Negative questions generally use **n't**. If **not** is used, there is a different word order:
  Shouldn't we leave? Should we not leave?

42 Modals

Check

Circle the correct word.

1   This is a no-smoking area. You (*mustn't*/won't) smoke here.

2   (*Can*/Ought) I help you?

3   It's very cold. You (*should*/will) wear a coat.

4   I can go home by train. You (*needn't*/couldn't) wait for me.

5   It's very cloudy. It (*might*/can) rain.

6   (*Could*/Must) you help me, please?

7   It's late. We (*ought to*/shall) go. → *debería*

no se pronuncia la "l"

8   It's eight o'clock. He (*will*/dare) be here soon. → *expresa seguridad de que pase algo*

9   (Would/*Shall*) I open the door for you?

10   She's busy at the moment. She (must/*may*) be late.

43   *can, could, be able to*: tense changes

- *be able to* is sometimes used instead of *can*:

Present	**can** or **am able to**
Past	**could** or **was able to**
Future	**can** or **will be able to**

[handwritten: = ser capaz de...]

Notes

- *can* indicates future when used with a time word.
- *be able to* is used in all tenses (**have been able to, had been able to**, etc.).
- For *can't have* and *couldn't have* ➤ Exercises 52 and 53.
- *could* and *was able to*:
  I could drive when I was eighteen.
  (= I knew how to.)
  I was able to drive to college because my uncle lent me a car for the year.
  (= I knew how to and I did it.)

Practice

In your notebook, write these sentences using the correct form of *can*, *could*, or *be able to*. Where two answers are possible, write them both.

1   I .... see you tomorrow.

   I'll be able to see you tomorrow.

   I can see you tomorrow.

2   It was too expensive – I .... buy it.

   It was too expensive – I couldn't buy it.

   It was too expensive – I wasn't able to buy it.

3   *[handwritten: Can]* .... I have a word with you, please?

4   I generally leave work at six, but I .... *[handwritten: am able to / or can]* leave earlier on Fridays.

5   *[handwritten: Can]* .... you help me carry this downstairs?

6   (she) *[handwritten: Can / Will she able to]* .... come to the office tomorrow?

7   I tried to see her, but I *[handwritten: couldn't or wasn't able to]* ....

8   It was so heavy that I *[handwritten: couldn't]* .... lift it. *[handwritten: levantar]*

9   I .... *[handwritten: will not be able to]* come tomorrow, I'm afraid. I'm too busy. *[handwritten: Pesado]*

10   (you) .... *[handwritten: were you able to or could you]* contact your parents yesterday?

11   He .... *[handwritten: hasn't been able to]* (not) work since his illness.

12   After I had tried for a few hours, I .... *[handwritten: could or was able to]* open the door and get out.

13   I .... *[handwritten: can / will be able to]* see you next Monday at ten.

14   They didn't come to the restaurant – they .... *[handwritten: couldn't]* (not) afford it.

15   When they came back from Paris they *[handwritten: could]* .... speak perfect French.

44 *must, have to*: positive and negative

- *must* and *have to* have similar meanings in the positive:
  You must leave. (= you can't stay) *You have to leave.* (= you can't stay)

- *must* and *have to* have different meanings in the negative:
  You mustn't leave. (= obligation – you can't go)
  You don't have to leave. (= no obligation – you can go or stay, as you like)

  ausencia de obligación

Notes

- *have to* is not a modal verb. It is included in this section because it often has the same meaning as *must*, and is used instead of *must* in some tenses (➤ Exercise 45). It forms questions and negatives in the same way as all other main verbs.

- *have got to* has the same meaning as *have to*:
  I've got to go. = I have to go.

Practice

Match the pairs of sentences which are closest in meaning.

1 You have to leave. ....7....
2 You don't have to leave. ..10...
3 You mustn't leave. 12...
4 You mustn't take the money. ...11...
5 You don't have to take the job. ..15...
6 You mustn't take the job. ..14...
7 You must go. ....1....
8 Must you go? ...13...
9 You don't have to take the money. ..16..
10 You can stay if you like. 2.....
11 Don't take the money. ...4...
12 You have to stay. ..3....
13 Do you have to go? ...8...
14 You definitely shouldn't take the job. ...6...
15 You can decide whether to take the job or not. ..5....
16 You can take the money or leave it, as you like. ..9......

si e

45 *must, have to*: tense changes

- *have to* is used instead of *must* in future and past tenses, and sometimes in the present.

Present	must or have to
Past	— had to
Present Perfect	— have had to
Future	— will have to

Notes

- *have to* can be used in all tenses.
- *must* sometimes indicates future when used with a time word:
  I must do this tomorrow morning.
- For *must have* ➤ Exercises 52 and 53.
- Note the different forms for questions and negatives:
  You mustn't leave.   *You don't have to leave.*
  Must you leave?   *Do you have to leave?*
- For the difference in meaning between *mustn't* and *don't have to* ➤ Exercise 44.

Practice

Put the correct form of *must* or *have to* in these sentences. Use the negative or question if necessary and put *have to* in the correct tense. In some sentences, two answers are possible.

1 I .*had to*. leave the party early last night – I wasn't very well.

2 I'm sorry, you *mustn't* smoke in here.

3 The children are happy because they ..*don't have to*.. do any homework today. *have to*

4 You ..*will must*... get up early tomorrow if you want to catch the bus. *Must you*

5 ..*Do you have to*..(you) have a visa to come here?

6 It was a very bad accident. You ..*will have to* be more careful in future.

7 He's been ill. He ..*has had to*.. stay in bed since last month.

8 I've told the children that they .....*must*....... come home before ten on Saturday nights. *have to*

9 *Did you have to*... (you) do military service in your country when you were young?

10 It was a lovely holiday. We ...*didn't have to* do anything.

11 They were very rude. They ......*had to*...... apologize the next day.

12 The teacher told us that we ...*had to*...... work harder.

13 You ...*must*............. get a passport before you go abroad next month.

14 We ...*had to*...... come back by boat because the airport was closed by fog.

15 You ...*mustn't*....... borrow my books without asking.

46   should, ought to

- **should** and **ought to** have similar meanings.
  ought to always uses **to**, **should** never uses **to**:
  We ought to stay here. We should stay here.
  Ought we to go? Should we go?
  You shouldn't make a noise in here.
  You oughtn't to make a noise in here.

Notes

- **should** / **ought to** are not as strong as **must** / **have to**:
  You must go now! (= you have no choice: go now)
  You should go now. (= it's your decision, but if I were you I would go now)

- Note the position of **to** in **ought to**:
  You ought to go home now.
  You oughtn't to go home now.
  Oughtn't you to go home now?

- **should** is used more often than **ought to**.

Practice

Write the second sentence, using **should** or **ought to** and the words given.

1   It's past the children's bedtime. (they / be / in bed)

   They should be in bed.

   They ought to be in bed.

2   Can't they see the 'No Smoking' sign? (they / not smoke / in here)

   They shouldn't smoke in here.

   They oughtn't to smoke in here.

3   These windows are dirty. (you / clean them / more often)

   ....

4   Peter drives too fast. (he / drive / more carefully)

   ...*he should drive more carefully*...............

5   He owes you a lot of money. (you / not lend him / any more)

   ...*You should not lend him any more*

6   There won't be much food at the party. (we / take something / to eat?)

   ...*Should we take something to eat!*

7   I'm not sure what to wear at the wedding. (I / wear / a suit?)

Should I wear a suit?

8   He says he can get us what we want. (we / pay him / now?)

Should we pay him now?

9   The hotel is too expensive. (we/not stay/there)

we shouldn't stay there

10 It's their wedding anniversary next week. (maybe we / send them / a present)

maybe we should send them a present

47   *should, ought to, must, have to*

- Advice or recommendation: *should* and *ought to* have similar meanings (➤ Exercise 46):
  You should tell your father about this problem.
  You ought to tell your father about this problem.

- Indicating a probable future event: *should* and *ought to* have similar meanings:
  They should be here soon.
  They ought to be here soon.

- In reported speech, *should* is used instead of *shall* (➤ Exercise 62):
  I asked if I should open the door.

- *must* and *have to* have similar meanings in the positive, but *must* is sometimes used to show a position of authority:
  Parent to child: '*You must be back by seven o'clock.*'
  (here, the authority comes from the speaker)
  One friend to another: '*You'll have to get up early to catch the morning train.*'
  (here, the obligation comes from the situation)

➤ Exercises 52 and 53 for past tenses.

Practice

Put *should, ought to, must* or *have to* in the sentences below, using negatives or questions if necessary. Sometimes more than one answer is possible, but you should write one only.

1   They *should / ought to* be arriving in a few hours.

2   We *have to* go home at twelve because my mother wants the car.

3   They insisted that we ....*should*.... have a meal.

4   There are no trains today, so we ......*have*...... to go by car.

5   I think you ....*should*.... tell your parents you're going to be late. They'll be worried.

6 You ...*must*...... never do that again!

7 The manager suggested that we ...*should*... try to find another hotel.

8 You ....*have to*...... see that film if you get the chance.

9 According to our information, the President ...*should*... be re-elected.

10 Do you think we ....*must*........ ask before we borrow the car?

11 You ...*don't have*... come if you don't want to.

12 You ....*mustn't*..... be smoking at your age.

13 He asked me anxiously what he ...*should*... do next.

14 Do you think I ...*should*... tell the teacher what happened?

15 My boss told me that I ...*mustn't*.... be late.

48 *need* + infinitive

- Positive:
  I need to practise my English.

- Negative:
  a) ***don't need to*** is generally used when the situation does not require something to be done:
     You don't need to have a visa to go to France from Britain.
  b) **needn't** is generally used when the speaker gives the authority for something not being done:
     Teacher to students: 'You needn't do any homework tonight.'

- Questions:
  a) *Do I need to apply for a visa?*
  b) *Need I do any homework this weekend?*

Note the use of *to* in the examples.

Practice

Write the correct form of ***need*** to complete these sentences.

1 The teacher says we *needn't* go to school tomorrow. (negative)

2 *Do* I *need to* have a licence to drive a car in this country? (question)

3 I've told her that she .... to work harder. (positive)

4 We .... take any equipment – the school provides it. (negative)

5 .... I .... phone you before I come to see you? (question)

6 My mother says I .... do the washing-up today. (negative)

69

7   You .... have more experience before you apply for this
    job. (positive)

8   You can go home now, you .... stay any longer.
    (negative)

9   You .... work here to be able to use the tennis court.
    (negative)

10 You .... say any more: I agree with you. (negative)

49   *need* as a main verb and *need* + gerund

- *need* can be used as a main verb:
  I need some petrol.
  Do you need anything else?

- *need* can be used with the gerund, with the same meaning as a passive
  construction.
  My car needs cleaning. (= My car needs to be cleaned.)
  Your hair needs washing. (= Your hair needs to be washed.)

Practice

Rewrite these sentences using *need* with an object or a gerund. It will be
necessary to change some words.

1   I think it's time for your house to be painted.

    Your house needs painting.

2   How many people should we have for a full team?

    How many people do we need for a full team?

3   There's a lot to do. We should have more time.

    ....

4   This floor is dirty: it should be cleaned immediately.

    ....

5   The doctor says that I should have more exercise.

    ....

6   Your tyres are very old. It's time to change them.

    ....

7   How much food should we have for the weekend?

    ....

8   How much money should we have for the trip?

    ....

9 The dog's hungry. It wants to be fed.

....

10 The baby's dirty. It's time to wash her.

....

50 *need* in the past

- Positive:
  I needed something to eat.
  I needed to rest for a few minutes.
  The house needed painting.

- Negative:
  a) **didn't need to** + infinitive
     I didn't need to get up early yesterday. (= it wasn't necessary, so I didn't)
  b) **needn't have** + past participle
     I needn't have got up early yesterday. (= it wasn't necessary, but I did it, and now I realise that it wasn't necessary)

Practice

Write **didn't need to** or **needn't have** and the correct form of the verb to complete these sentences.

1 I *didn't need to catch* (catch) the bus this morning, because Vic gave me a lift.

2 I *needn't have lent* (lend) him that money. I found out later that he had already borrowed all the money he wanted.

3 I .... (do) that homework – the teacher didn't even look at it.

4 I .... (take) a tent, because I knew I could hire one at the campsite.

5 You .... (buy) such an expensive present, but I'm very glad that you did.

6 I .... (take) any money: they had already told me that it wasn't necessary.

7 I .... (count) the money: they had already told me that it was done automatically.

8 I .... (work) so hard for my exams: they were much easier than I expected them to be.

9 I .... (get up) so early: I had forgotten it was
Saturday.

10 I had some friends in the town, so I ....
(stay) in a hotel.

51 *need*

In your notebook, put the verbs in the sentences below into the correct form,
adding *to* where necessary.

1 I (*not need / fix*) my bike yesterday – I could have used my father's.

   I needn't have fixed my bike yesterday – I could have used my father's.

2 I think the house (*need / paint*) now.

   I think the house needs painting now.

3 You're never here when I (*need*) you.

   You're never here when I need you.

4 You (*not need / stay*) any longer, boys – you can go home now.

5 How much money (*I need*) for the weekend?

6 I (*not need / take*) the car – we could have used Jenny's.

7 I (*not need / get up*) early yesterday – I forgot it was Saturday.

8 The room's rather dirty, I'm afraid – it (*need / clean*).

9 I stopped at the hotel because I (*need / have*) a rest.

10 You (*not need / send*) it by post – I could have picked it up.

11 Pat's a clever student, but she (*need / work*) harder.

12 The prisoners were told that they (*not need / do*) any more work.

13 There were no customs officers, so we (*not need / show*) our passports.

14 (*you need / have*) a special licence to drive a lorry?

15 You (*not need / worry*) Peter, everything will be all right.

52 Modals in the past tense

FORM

modal + **have** + past participle			
I He She It We You They	should could may might would must ought to can't	have	known. arrived. gone.

- Positive:
  I should have known.
  He might have arrived.
  They ought to have gone.

- Question:
  Should I have known?
  Ought they to have gone?
  Could he have arrived?

- Negative:
  I shouldn't have gone.
  He couldn't have known.
  They oughtn't to have gone.

Note: *have* stays the same for all persons (*he, she,* etc.), as this is the perfect infinitive.
(➤ Exercise 60).

Practice

Put these sentences into the past, using the perfect infinitive.

1 You shouldn't say that.

   You shouldn't have said that.

2 They might not go.

   They might not have gone.

3 She couldn't know.

   ....

4 The machine ought to work.

   ....

5 They can't leave.

   ....

6 We ought to stop them.

....

7 Should I tell the teacher?

....

8 Could they help me?

....

9 Ought I to stay?

....

10 He can't be there.

....

11 They might not like it.

....

12 He may agree.

....

13 Shouldn't he say something?

....

14 Couldn't John drive the car?

....

15 Shouldn't he check the information?

....

53   Modals in the past tense: different meanings

- *should* and *ought to* have their normal meaning in the past.
  You shouldn't have done that.
  You ought to have warned me about him.

- *may* and *might* have their normal meaning in the past.
  John might have told Mrs Jones what happened.
  Sheila may have left two or three days ago.

- *could* and *must* in the past are used to indicate deduction. *must have* is more certain than *could have*:
  Mike could have stayed in this hotel. (= it is possible that he stayed in this hotel)
  Mike must have stayed in this hotel. (= it is almost definite that he stayed in this hotel)

- *can't have* and *couldn't have* indicate a negative deduction. They are used as the negative for *must have*:

Mike can't have stayed in this hotel. (= it is almost definite that he didn't stay in this hotel)

- *could have* = it was possible, but I didn't do it:
  I could have left at ten o'clock, but I didn't.

Note: In the present, *must be, have to be, could be* and *can't be* can indicate deduction:
  He's late – something must be wrong!
  ➤ Exercise 45 for *had to*.
  ➤ Exercise 43 for *was able to*.
  ➤ Exercise 50 for *need* in the past.
  ➤ Exercise 37 for *could have, would have,* and *might have* in the conditional.

Practice

Put *could, must, should, might,* or *can't* in the past tense in the spaces provided. Sometimes more than one answer is possible:

1 How did you know about the wedding? Someone *must have told* (tell) you!

2 The money was on the desk: I *could have taken* (take) it, but I didn't.

3 I know you were angry, but you .... (not be) so rude.

4 I don't know who sent these flowers: it .... (be) Jane.

5 She .... (not move) abroad – she hates foreign countries.

6 .... (you not be) just a little more polite?

7 They .... (not know) about the plans for the new factory – it's not possible.

8 I think you .... (tell) your parents you were going to be late. They were very worried.

9 They .... (not get) into the house through a window: they were all closed.

10 They .... (not leave) without being seen by anybody.

11 I .... (go) for a swim if I'd wanted to.

12 You .... (apologize) for being late.

13 We don't know who took the money. The office was full of people and it
.... (be) any of them.

14 I .... (not say) such a terrible thing.

15 I .... (not leave) my keys at home – I'm sure they
were in my pocket.

16 He .... (warn) us that he was going to leave his job.

17 She tried to contact me, but the phone .... (be)
engaged.

18 He .... (not know) about her illness – nobody had
told him about it.

19 I don't know who wrote the letter. It .... (not be)
Mrs Johnson, as she wasn't in the office that day.

20 I'm sorry, I .... (let) you know what was
happening.

54   *could, would, might*

- + infinitive
  could = ability or possibility in the present or future:
  I could do it if you wanted me to.
  would = conditional intention in the present or future:
  I would do it if I were able to.
  might = possibility in the present or future:
  I might do it.

- + perfect infinitive
  could = ability or possibility in the past:
  He could have gone early, but he didn't.
  would = intention in the past:
  He would have gone early if they had let him.
  might = possibility in the past:
  He might have gone early – I don't know.

- Indirect speech:
  can → ***could***: *We knew that he could be annoying.*
  will → ***would***: *We knew that he would be annoying.*
  may/might → ***might***: *We knew that he might be annoying.*

- Requests:
  Could ⎫
  Would ⎭ *you open the door for me, please?*

- Offers:
  Could *I do it for you?*

Practice

Put *could*, *would*, or *might* in the correct form to complete these sentences.

1 I *might have* seen Janice at the party last night. What does she look like?

2 I'm sure I (not) *wouldn't have* done it if I hadn't been so angry.

3 We thought that he *could/would/might* be disappointed.

4 I .... give it to her tomorrow.

5 I .... be a bit more careful if I were you.

6 The train .... be an hour or two late.

7 You (not) .... been at the restaurant yesterday – I looked everywhere for you.

8 Put some food in your bag – the journey .... take hours.

9 She told me that the children .... be very noisy in the evening.

10 I thought that the shop .... be closed by seven o'clock.

11 .... you work if you weren't paid for it?

12 We didn't know what the noise was – it .... been anything.

13 I .... spoken to your boss if I'd seen her.

14 There .... be several reasons for the accident.

15 By half-past eight I knew that she (not) .... come.

16 .... you hold my coat for a minute?

17 Be careful when you go abroad – anything .... happen.

18 I .... said I was sorry, but I didn't.

19 They warned me that I .... not get the job.

20 .... I ask you a few questions?

Gerunds and infinitives

55 Gerund or infinitive?

REMEMBER!

The gerund
We use the gerund like a noun. We can use it in the following ways:
- As the subject of a verb:
  Swimming is very good for you.

- As an object after certain verbs:
  Have you finished working?

- After a preposition:
  Before leaving the house, she checked all the windows.

The infinitive
We can use the infinitive in the following ways.
- After certain verbs:
  I hope to be there before dark.

- To express purpose:
  I got up early to do my homework.

Check

Put the verbs in brackets into the gerund or the infinitive.

1 I want ..*to finish*.. (finish) work early tonight.

2 I hate ..*waiting*... (wait) for buses in the rain.

3 I'm going to the cafe ..*to meet*.... (meet) Alex.

4 Sam is really good at ..*climbing*... (climb).

5 I really need ..*to have*.... (have) a holiday soon.

6 ..*Parking*.... (park) a car in the centre of town is always really difficult.

7 We miss ..*living*.......... (live) by the sea.

8 Thank you for ....*being*...... (be) so helpful.

9 Don't forget ..*to lock*..... (lock) the door.

10 I enjoy ..*listening*... (listen) to the radio while I'm doing the cooking.

11 ..*Sharing*.... (share) a flat with friends is cheaper than ..*living*.. (live) alone.

12 Let's go now. I'm worried about ..*missing*.... (miss) the train.

13 It was getting dark when we finished ..*to play*...... (play) football.

14 They've worked very hard ..*to get*..... (get) this party ready.

15 He refused ..*to help*... (help) me.

56 Person + gerund

- In formal English, possessive + gerund can be used:
  *I have no objection to **your arriving** late.*
  *We are concerned about **the company's trading** in oil.*

- In conversational English, the possessive is not used: the object form is used instead:
  *I don't mind **him coming** late.*
  *We are worried about **Jane working** so hard.*

Practice

Write both the possessive and object form of the words provided.

1 I don't like *your/you* asking him to stay. (you)

2 Do you mind *my/me* smoking? (I)

3 The shareholders agreed to *our / ours* closing down the factory. (we)

4 They don't understand *Johns/John* leaving home when he did. (John)

5 I'm worried about *her / her* taking so much money. (she)

6 I didn't like *your / your* lending the car to him. (you)

7 The board objected to *Mr Maslin* resigning. (Mr Maslin)

8 I'm bored with *theirs/them* complaining. (they)

9 Do you know the reason for *them / their* stopping work? (they)

10 Who told you about *him/his* being sacked? (he)

11 What do you think of *them / their* leaving the country like that? (they)

12 I can think of no reason for *her/her* saying that. (she)

13 They approved of *him / his* reorganizing the working day. (he)

14 The company did not mind *us/our* spending the money. (we)

15 The new proposals involve *my/me* working longer hours. (I)

57 *to* + infinitive after nouns and adjectives

to + infinitive can be used
- after certain adjectives:
  I was pleased to see them again.
  I'm surprised to hear you say that.

   Note the expression *too* ... *to*:
   It was too hot to go out.

- after certain nouns and pronouns, to show what is to be done with them or how they are to be used:
  I've got some homework to do.
  Is there anyone else to see?

   Note the expression *enough* ... *to*:
   Have we got enough money to go to the cinema?

Practice

Put the words in the correct order to make sentences, making one verb an infinitive and writing the other in the present simple.

1 plane catch she a have.

   She has a plane to catch.

2 lot of a housework there be do.

   There is a lot of housework to do.

3 who something eat want?

   Who want something to eat?

4 smoke he young be too.

   he is too young to smoke

5 come expect Jane I.

   I except Jane to come

6 delighted hear I be the news.

   I'm delighted the news to hear

7 have books some I read.

   I have books to read

8 illness surprised hear I be his of.

   I'm surprised to hear of illness

9 nothing children the have do.

   The children have nothing to do

10 letters I write some have.

   I have some letter to write

11 shopping some he do have.

He has some shopping to do

12 nothing say have I.

I have nothing to say

13 always much eat have you too to.

You always have too much to eat

14 outside cold eat it too be.

It too cold outside to eat

15 lovely see it again you be.

It's lovely to see you your again

58   *it* + *to* + **infinitive**

to + infinitive is used
- after *that / it / there* + *to be* + adjective + noun:
  *That was a stupid thing **to do**.*
  *It was a strange thing **to say**.*
  *There are other people **to see**.*

- after *it* + *to be* + adjective. This sometimes uses *of you*, *of him*, etc.:
  *It was nice **of you to come**.*
  *It was kind **of them to send** me money.*
  *It was good **to see** them again.*
  *It was difficult **to drive** the car with one hand.*

Practice

Rewrite these sentences, starting with the words given. You will need to change some words.

1 Why did he ask that question? It was very strange.

   That *was a very strange question to ask.*

2 Thank you for visiting Janice in hospital. It was very kind.

   It *was very kind of you to visit Janice in hospital.*

3 Why did he make that remark? It was very rude.

   That *was very rude to make that remark*

4 I enjoyed flying the plane. It was very exciting.

   It *was very exciting to fly the plane*

5 I'm pleased I saw her again. It was quite a surprise.

   It *was quite a surprise to see her again*

6 John gave them £100. It was very generous.

   It *was very generous of John*

7   I couldn't drive the car. It was very difficult.

It *was very difficult to drive the car*

8   Why did you visit that place? It was very odd.

That *was very odd place to visit*

9   Why did he do that? It was very silly.

It *was very silly thing to do*

10 He shouldn't have driven the car like that. It was stupid.

It *was stupid to drive the car like that* of him to drive the car

59   Use of the infinitive without *to*

The infinitive without *to* is used:
- after *will*, *can*, *must*, etc.

- after *make* and *let* + noun/pronoun:
  *He made me **do** it.*
  *We let them **go** home.*

- after verbs of seeing, hearing and feeling + noun/pronoun:
  *I saw him **arrive**.*
  *We watched them **go**.*
  *I felt him **move**.*

Note: Verbs of seeing, hearing or feeling can also use the present participle:
  *I saw him **arrive**.*
  *I saw him **arriving**.*

Practice

Rewrite the sentences, using the words given.

1   He arrived early. (I saw)

I saw him arrive early.

2   I didn't want to stay at home. (They made me)

They made me stay at home.

3   She got out of the car. (We watched)

We watched her get out of the car

4   They allowed me to telephone my lawyer. (They let)

they let me telephone my lawyer

5   They left at eleven o'clock. (I heard)

I heard them leave at eleven o'clock

6   The policeman told me to empty my pockets. (The policeman made)

The policeman made me empty my pockets

7 The dog jumped through the window. (I saw)

I saw the dog jump through the window.

8 Maybe the school will ask me to pay extra. (Do you think the school will make)

Do you think the school will make me pay extra?

9 The animal moved. I felt it. (I felt the)

I felt the animal move.

10 I want to leave the country. (Do you think the government will let)

Do you think the government will let me leave the country?

60 The perfect infinitive

FORM

- The perfect infinitive is formed with **have** + past participle:
  go → have gone or *to have gone*
  see → have seen or *to have seen*

USE

- in the third conditional (➤ Exercise 37) with **would**, **might** or **could**:
  If he'd phoned, I would have met him at the airport.

- with **could**, **must**, **need**, **can't**, **might**, etc. in the past (➤ Exercise 53)
  Who could have told him the news?

- after verbs such as **want**, **expect** and **hope** as a future perfect: This form uses **to**:
  I hope to have finished this by Christmas.

- after certain adjectives, as a past. This form uses **to**:
  I was disappointed to have missed him.

Practice

Put the verbs in brackets into the perfect infinitive. Use *to* where necessary.

1   I expect .*to have finished* (finish) working here by the end of the year.

2   They can't .*have known* (know) what was going to happen.

3   The children are very pleased .... (finally meet) their uncle.

4   We hope .... (contact) all the record manufacturers in Britain when we finish the survey.

5   I expect .... (collect) £3,000 by this time next year.

6   If I'd known he was in hospital, I would .... (visit) him.

7   I was disappointed .... (miss) such a good opportunity.

8   I want .... (finish) the job by the time I go home.

9   We were very pleased .... (be able to) help.

10 Lots of people could .... (tell) the newspapers what had happened.

61   Gerund or infinitive?

CONTRAST

- some verbs use only the gerund, and some verbs use only the infinitive. Certain verbs use either. (➤ Exercise 30 for a full list).

- The gerund is used:
  a) after prepositions:
     *We talked **about cooking**.*
  b) as a verbal noun:
     ***Swimming** is excellent exercise.*
  c) after certain expressions such as **can't stand**, **can't bear**, etc.
     *I **can't stand going** to the dentist.*

- The infinitive is used:
  a) after certain nouns or adjectives (➤ Exercise 57)
  b) to express purpose:
     *I came here **to study**.*
  c) after **it** + **to be** + adjective/noun (➤ Exercise 58)

- Some verbs (e.g. *love*, *hate*, *start*, *prefer*) can take gerund or infinitive, with similar meanings:
  I love to visit old houses.
  I love visiting old houses.
  I started to polish the car, but then decided not to.
  I started polishing the car, but then decided not to.

  [handwritten: se pueden decir las dos cosas.]

- *remember*, *stop*, and *try* have a different meaning with the gerund or the infinitive:

  [handwritten: Recuerdas que tienes que hacer algo.]

  a) *I remembered to give him the money.*
     (= the remembering happened before the giving)
     I remembered giving him the money.

     [handwritten: Interrumpir la actividad que estas haciendo en este momento.]

     (= the remembering happened after the giving)
  b) *I stopped to watch the carnival.*
     (= I stopped because I wanted to watch the carnival)
     I stopped watching the carnival.
     (= I had been watching the carnival: then I stopped watching)
  c) *I tried to open the door, but it was locked.*
     (= I didn't open it)
     I tried opening the door to let in some fresh air.
     (= I did open it)

Practice

Put the verb in the gerund or the infinitive.

1 *Flying* is really good fun. (fly)

2 We stopped at the motorway services *to get* something *to eat*. (get/eat)

3 'What's this for?'
   'It's for *cooking* vegetables.' (cook)

4 I can't get used to *getting up* before the dawn. (get up)

5 I'm sorry about *not inviting* you. (not invite)

6 There's a lot of work *doing* on the new building. (do)

7 I really love *playing* with the children. (play)

8 *Swimming* is a good form of exercise. (swim)

9 There are some very interesting things *to see* in the British Museum. (see)

10 You're lucky you haven't got a child .... (look after)

11 We managed .... the exam by .... each other every evening. (pass/test)

12 Dave decided .... Sheila for a week or two. (not phone)

13 I can't stand .... the washing-up. (do)

14 I think I'm going to have to give up .... football. (play)

15 It really is time .... (go)

16 I've decided .... here for another year. (not stay)

17 I know the keys are here: I remember .... somewhere. (put them down)

18 We were getting tired, so we stopped .... lunch. (have)

19 I tried .... some salt, but it didn't help. (add)

20 I'm looking forward to .... the programme. (see)

21 I went home .... that the children were all right. (check)

22 You're much too young .... in there. (go)

23 I was surprised .... about the new baby. (not hear)

24 We're very keen on .... the team. (join)

25 It was a very odd thing .... (say)

26 We decided .... until the end of the film. (not stay)

27 I miss .... to see my parents every day. (be able)

28 They wouldn't let me .... in the driving-seat (sit)

29 It's your last chance .... you're sorry. (say)

30 We agreed .... any more work. (not do)

Reported speech

62 Reported statements: tense changes

- When the main verb of the sentence is in the past tense, the tense in the reported statement is changed.

'I'll talk to Mr Jones.'   → *He said he'd talk to Mr Jones.*
'I haven't seen anybody.' → *She said she hadn't seen anybody.*
'I must go.'   → *He said he had to go.*

- Tense changes when the main verb is past tense:

Speaker's words	Reported statement
will →	*would*
shall →	*should*
is going to →	*was going to*
present simple →	*past simple*
present continuous →	*past continuous*
past continuous →	*past perfect continuous*
present perfect ⎱→ *past simple* ⎰	*past perfect*
must →	*had to*
can →	*could*

- **that** is optional after the main verb:
  *He said **that** he wasn't going.*
  He said he wasn't going.

Practice

Write these sentences in indirect speech.

1 'I'm very tired,' she said.

   She said she was very tired.

2 'I'll see them soon,' he said.

   He said he would see them soon.

3 'I'm going to the cinema,' she said.

   She said she was going to the cinema

4 'I see the children quite often,' he said.

He said he saw the children quite often

5 'I'm having a bath,' she said.

She said she was having a bath

6 'I've already met their parents,' he said.

He said he had already met their parents

7 'I stayed in a hotel for a few weeks,' she said.

She said she had stayed in a hotel for a few weeks

8 'I must go home to make the dinner,' he said.

He said he had to go home to make the dinner

9 'I haven't been waiting long,' she said.

She said she hadn't been waiting long

10 'I'm listening to the radio,' he said.

He said he was listening to the radio

11 'I'll tell them the news on Saturday,' she said.

She said she would them the news on Saturday

12 'I like swimming, dancing and playing tennis,' he said.

He said he liked swimming etc

13 'I can drive,' she said.

She said she could drive

14 'I walked home after the party,' he said.

He said he had walked home after the party

15 'I'm going to be sick,' she said.

She said she was going to be sick

16 'I must go out to post a letter,' he said.

He said he had to go out to post a letter

17 'I spoke to Jane last week,' she said.

She said she had spoken to Jane last week

18 I'm trying to listen to the music,' he said.

He said he was trying to listen to the music

19 'I'll phone the office from the airport,' she said.

She said she would phone

20 'I can't speak any foreign languages,' he said.

He said He couldn't speak

63 Reported statements: other changes

- As well as tense changes (➤ Exercise 62), other words in direct speech need to be changed when they are reported. Here are some examples:

Speaker's words	Reported statement
tomorrow → the next day/the following day
yesterday → the day before
here → there
this/that → the
this morning → that morning
today → that day
tonight → that night
next/on Tuesday → the following Tuesday
last Tuesday → the previous Tuesday
the day after tomorrow → in two days' time
ago → before/previously

- Note that these changes generally occur, but they are not automatic. They depend on when and where the statement is reported.

- Some verbs do not change:
  would → would, could → could, might → might
  should → should, ought to → ought to

Practice

Write these sentences in indirect speech, changing words where necessary.

1 'I'll see you tomorrow,' she said.

   She said she'd see me the next day.

2 'I saw her today,' he said.

   He said he'd seen her that day.

3 'I don't like this film,' she said.

   ....

4 She said, 'We went swimming today.'

   ....

5 'I'll see Mary on Sunday,' she said.

   ....

6 'I met her about three months ago,' he said.

   ....

7 'Pete and Sue are getting married tomorrow,' she said.

   ....

   ....

8 'Stephen's bringing some records to the party tonight,' he said.

....

....

9 'I really like this furniture,' she said.

....

10 'My parents are arriving tomorrow,' she said.

....

11 'We visited her this morning,' they said.

....

12 'We'll see her next week,' they said.

....

13 'They were here three months ago,' he said.

....

14 'I'm meeting them at four o'clock today,' he said.

....

....

15 'I can see you tomorrow,' she said.

....

64 Reported questions: *wh* questions

- Most reported questions have a main verb in the past tense. They use the same tense changes and word changes as in reported statements (➤ Exercises 62 and 63).

- Reported questions change the word order of the original question:
  'What's the time?'
  She asked what time it was.
  (NOT ~~She asked what was the time.~~)

  'How's your mother?'
  He asked me how my mother was.
  (NOT ~~He asked me how was my mother.~~)

Note: *ask* can be used in reported speech with or without a personal direct object:
  She asked me how I was.
  She asked how I was.

Practice

Write these sentences as reported questions, using the words given. Change *you* to *I*, etc. where necessary.

1 'What's your name?' he asked. (wanted to know)

   He wanted to know what my name was.

2 'How old are you?' she said. (asked)

   She asked how old I was.

3 'When does the train leave?' I asked. (asked)

   I asked When the train left?

4 'How are you?' he said. (asked)

   He asked How I was

5 'Who did you see at the meeting?' my mother said. (wanted to know)

   My mother wanted to know who I had seen at the meeting

6 'Why did you take my wallet?' he asked. (wanted to know)

   He wanted to know Why he had taken his wallet

7 'How did you get to school?' she said. (asked)

   She asked how he had gotten to school

8 'Where do you live?' the boy asked. (wanted to know)

   the boy wanted to know where he had lived

9 'Why wasn't Judy at the party?' she asked. (asked)

   She asked Why Judy hadn't been at the party

10 'Why didn't you telephone?' my father asked. (wanted to know)

    My father wanted to know why I hadn't telephone

11 'Why are you so late?' the teacher asked. (demanded to know)

    the teacher demanded to know why I was so late

12 'Why didn't the police report the crime?' the judge asked. (inquired)

    the judge asked why the police hadn't been report the crime

13 'Why won't you let me in?' he shouted. (demanded to know)

He demanded to know why I wouldn't let me in

14 'What time does the plane arrive?' we asked. (inquired)

We inquired what time the plane arrived

15 'Who do you want to talk to?' she said. (asked)

She asked who I wanted to talk to

65 Reported questions: *if / whether*

- *if* or *whether* (the choice is optional) is used for reported questions that do not start with *wh* words (➤ Exercise 64).
  *He asked **if** I was hungry.*
  Note the word order change:
  '***Are you** angry?*' → *He asked if **I was** angry.*
  '***Did you see** the film?*' → *She asked whether **I had seen** the film.*

- Tense changes and other word changes are as shown in Exercises 62 and 63.

Practice

Write these sentences as reported questions. Change *you* to *I*, etc. where necessary.

1 'Do you like Marlon Brando?' she asked.

   She asked if I liked Marlon Brando.

2 'Are you enjoying yourself?' he asked.

   He asked whether I was enjoying myself.

3 'Does your father work here?' she asked.

   She asked if my father worked here

4 'Do you live near your family?' he asked.

   He asked whether he lived near your family

5 'Are you a foreigner?' she asked.

   She asked whether/if I was a foreigner

6 'Have you met Danny before?' he asked.

   He asked whether/if I had met Danny before

7 'Are you hungry?' she asked.

   She asked whether/if I was hungry

8 'Did you borrow my dictionary?' he asked.

....

9 'Have you finished your exams?' she asked.

....

10 'Did you invite Judy and Pat?' he asked.

....

11 'Does your brother live in London?' she asked.

....

12 'Do you know who broke the window?' he asked.

....

....

13 'Did they tell you when they were leaving?' she asked.

....

14 'Did you lend them your camera?' he asked.

....

15 'Have you hurt yourself?' she asked.

....

66 Reported questions

Check

Write these sentences in indirect speech, using **wanted to know** and the words given. Change **you** to **I**, etc. where necessary, as in the examples.

1 'Which book did you take?' (he)

He wanted to know which book I had taken.

2 'Are you wearing your overcoat?' (she)

She wanted to know if/whether I was wearing my overcoat.

3 'Did you telephone your mother?' (he)

He asked if/whether I telephoned your mother

4 'Is the box made of cardboard?' (she)

She asked if/whether the box was made of cardboard

5 'How much did it cost? (he)

He asked How much it had cost

6 'Are you seeing the director tomorrow?' (she)

She asked whether if I was seeing the director Tomorrow

7 'What are you doing?' (he)

he asked what I was doing

8 'How far do I have to walk?' (she)

She asked How far I had to walk

9 'Have you had anything to eat?' (he)

He asked if/whether I had had anything to eat

10 'Are you in a hurry?' (she)

She asked if/whether I was in a hurry

11 'When does the performance start?' (he)

He asked when the performance started

12 'How long does the journey take?' (she)

She asked How long the journey taked

13 'Where did you stay in Paris?' (he)

he asked where I had stayed in Paris

14 'Have you had any letters?' (she)

She asked whether I had had any letters

15 'Do you like having holidays abroad?' (he)

He asked if/whether I liked having holidays abroad

16 'Did you see the accident?' (she)

she asked if/whether I had seen the accident

17 'Which school did you go to?' (he)

He asked which I had gone to school

18 'When did you start learning Spanish?' (she)

She asked when I had started learning Spanish

19 'Are you French?' (he)

He asked if/whether French I was

20 'Have you ever been to Japan?' (she)

She asked if/whether I had ever been to Japan

67 Reported commands

- Reported commands use a personal direct object and the infinitive:

He told the children to stop.

He told them to stop.

- The negative uses **not** before **to** + infinitive:
  'Don't stop!' → *He told them not to stop.*
  'Don't go!' → *He told me not to go.*

- A number of verbs can be used for reported commands; e.g. **tell**, **order**, **command**, **warn**, **instruct**, etc.

➤ Exercise 68 for reported requests.

Practice

Write these sentences in indirect speech, using the words given. Note that some words may have to be changed.

1 'Sit down Mary.' (he told)

   He told Mary to sit down.

2 'Don't go near the sea, children.' (the children's mother warned)

   The children's mother warned them not to go near the sea.

3 'Don't be late, Tim.' (Tim's father told)

   ....

4 'Be quiet, children.' (the librarian told)

   ....

5 'Don't shoot, men!' (the officer ordered)

   ....

6 'Have your tickets ready, please.' (the inspector told us)

   ....

   ....

7 'Don't use the telephone after eleven o'clock.' (the landlady told us)

....

....

8 'Leave your keys on the desk, please.' (the receptionist told us)

....

....

9 'Have your passports ready, please.' (the customs officer told us)

....

....

10 'Finish the job tonight, please.' (my boss told me)

....

....

11 'Run!' (the general ordered the soldiers)

....

12 'Open the door, please.' (my mother told me)

....

13 'Don't spend too much money on your holiday.' (my father told me)

....

....

14 'Hurry up.' (he told me)

....

15 'Don't be frightened.' (she told me)

....

68   Reported requests

- Reported requests (when you are asking someone to do something for you) have the same grammatical form as reported commands (➤ Exercise 67):
  'Would you open the door, please?'
  → *She asked me to open the door.*
  'Could you lend me some money, please?'
  → *He asked me to lend him some money.*

- Reported requests usually use **ask** as the main verb. There is an important difference in meaning between:
  *He **told** me to give him some money.* and
  *He **asked** me to give him some money.*

Note the difference between a reported offer and a reported request.
   a) offer:
      'Would you like a cigarette?'
      → *He asked if I would like a cigarette.*
   b) request:
      'Would you pass me a cigarette?'
      → *He asked me to pass him a cigarette.*

Practice

Write these sentences in indirect speech.

1   'Would you pass my suitcase, please?' he asked.

   He asked me to pass his suitcase.

2   'Would you like some coffee?' she asked.

   She asked if I would like some coffee.

3   'Would you take the children to school for me?' he asked.

   ....

   ....

4   'Would you sit down, please?' she asked.

   ....

   ....

5   'Would you talk more quietly, please?' he asked.

   ....

   ....

6   'Would you like a lift into town?' she asked.

   ....

   ....

7 'Would you like to go out at the weekend?' he asked.

....

....

8 'Would you turn on the radio, please?' she asked.

....

....

9 'Would you move your car, please?' he asked.

....

....

10 'Would you like to eat in the hotel or in a restaurant?' she asked.

....

....

11 'Would you pass my cup, please?' he asked.

....

....

12 'Would you check the oil for me, please?' she asked.

....

....

13 'Would you turn the car engine off, please?' he asked.

....

....

14 'Would you like to stay with us?' she asked.

....

....

15 'Would you check the bill for me, please?' he asked.

....

....

69 Indirect speech

Check

Complete these sentences with the correct form of the verbs.

1 He said he _had_ already _spoken_ to the manager. (speak)

2 She asked me _to take off_ my shoes. (take off)

3 He wanted to know where I _had been living_ for the last few years. (live)

4 I warned her _not to go_ too near the cliff edge. (not go)
borde del precipicio

5 I asked her if Mrs Brownlow _had_ just _left_ . (leave)

6 I told them _to check_ they were in the right part of the train. (check)

7 He told me he _haven't eaten_ for several days. (not eat)

8 We agreed that I _would see_ them a few days later. (see)

9 They asked me if I _would like_ a cup of tea. (like)

10 He begged her _to give_ him some money, but she refused. (give)
2055

11 The police ordered the crowd _to stay back_ . (stay back)

12 She wants to know if the manager _will come back_ tomorrow. (come back)

13 The expression on his face told me that I _was_ late. (be)

14 We decided that the computer _had to be_ switched off. (have to be)

15 We advised the company _to open_ a new factory. (open)

16 I asked him whether Mr Steadman _had registered_ yet. (register)
matricularse

17 He ordered his soldiers _to stay_ there. (stay)

18 Your parents want to know if you _having_ a good time at the moment. (have)

19 They told me that the train _was leaving_ at that very moment. (leave)

20 I wanted to know how much money I _had_ in my bank account. (have)

21 Mr Jones wants to know why you suddenly _decided_ to resign last week. (decide)

22 The other people in the flat asked me ...*not to smoke*... (not smoke)

23 The publishers have told me that they *~~are~~ not to going to accept* my book. (not going to accept)

24 She replied that she ...*didn't know*...... the answer. (not know)

25 They told me I ...*hadn't been*...... very polite the previous evening. (not be)

26 He indicated that he ....*agreed*............... by nodding his head. (agree)

27 They shouted that they ....*couldn't*........... cross the river and that they .*were going to go*. back to the car. (cannot / going to go)

28 They asked me ...*not to say*......... anything but just ......*listen*............... quietly. (not say / listen)

29 She asked when the plane ..*had arrived*........ the night before and whether it ..*had come*........... direct from Brussels. (arrive / come)

30 He asked whether I ...*had talked*...... to Dr Jones when I was in hospital. (talk)

70 Verbs used in reporting

- It is not always necessary to report all the words a person says: some verbs are used to provide a summary instead:
  'Oh, dear,' she said, 'I'm terribly sorry I'm late.'
  → *She apologized for being late.*
  'Yes, you're right. I was very foolish', he said.
  → *He agreed that he had been very foolish.*

- The verbs are followed by the infinitive, gerund, or indirect speech.

Practice

Rewrite these sentences, choosing the correct verb from the box for each sentence and using it with the construction shown. In some cases the verb may replace part of the sentence. Use each verb once only.

> Verbs that take the infinitive:
> **advise, invite, offer, promise, refuse, remind, warn**
>
> Verbs that take the gerund:
> **apologise for, insist on, suggest**
>
> Verbs followed by indirect speech:
> **agree, ~~announce~~, boast, claim, concede**

1 'We're going to get married in June,' she said.

She announced that they were going to get married in June.

2 'Don't go near that dog,' she told him.

....

3 After the meal, he said, 'Please don't argue – I'm going to pay.'

....

4 'I'm sorry I didn't write,' she said.

....

5 'Would you like to come round for dinner on Friday evening?' he asked them.

....

6 'I think you should give up smoking,' the doctor said to her.

....

7 'Alright, yes, I was wrong and you were right,' he said.

....

8 'Yes, I'll write every week,' she said.

....

9 'Shall I carry that suitcase for you?' she said.

....

10 'How about going to the theatre on Saturday?' he said.

....

11 'The newspaper report's not true,' said the Prime Minister.

....

12 'Don't forget to post that letter,' she said to him.

....

13 'Yes, it was a difficult exam,' the teacher said.

....

14 'No, I won't give you a pay rise,' the manager told her.

....

15 'My parents have got three cars,' she said.

....

71   Reporting conversations: summarising

- When we report conversations, we do not normally report everything that was said; we select the important parts. This is part of a 'phone conversation between Anne and Sue:

ANNE: Are you doing anything at the weekend?
SUE: No, we're not.
ANNE: Well, would you like to come and stay with us for the weekend? I know you're all in need of a rest.
SUE: Oh, that would be lovely! Thank you very much.
ANNE: Not at all, it will be nice to see you again.
SUE: The only problem is, I haven't told you yet, but we bought a dog last week.
ANNE: A dog! How nice!
SUE: Yes ... we can leave him with Paul's parents.
ANNE: No, no, bring him. I'd love to see him.
SUE: No, I couldn't possibly. He's rather young and playful, and he might start eating your furniture!
ANNE: That doesn't matter, really. You know I like dogs, so do bring him.
SUE: Are you sure?
ANNE: Yes, of course.
SUE: Oh well, in that case I will ...

This is how Sue described the conversation to her husband Paul:

'Anne has invited us to stay with her for the weekend. She thought we needed a rest! I explained that we'd bought a dog and said that we could leave him with your parents, but she insisted that we should bring him.'

Practice

Below is a conversation between Jane and David. Jane later describes the conversation to her husband Peter. In your notebook, write what she said, starting with: *'Oh, I saw David today. He ...'*

There are several ways of summarizing the conversation.

JANE   My parents are coming this weekend. I don't know what we're going to do with them.
DAVID: Why don't you take them to that new French restaurant in town, 'Le Pain'? It really is good, honestly. Jackie and I went there last week and the food was fantastic. I'm sure your parents would like it. *the week before*
JANE: Mm, that's a good idea. Do you think they'd let children in there?
DAVID: Oh, I think so. But why don't you leave the kids with us? Jackie and I would be happy to look after them. We're not going anywhere on Saturday night.   *cuidan niños*
JANE: Well, that's very nice of you. Are you really sure that would be OK?
DAVID: Of course I'm sure.
JANE: Well, that's marvellous! We'll bring them round to you at about 7.30. I hope they won't give you any trouble ...
DAVID: Of course they won't. they can try out the new computer.
JANE: Have you got a new computer? Jackie didn't say anything about that ...

DAVID: Do you remember she was applying for a job with the BBC? Well, she got it – and the computer comes with the job.

JANE: She got the job? That's great news!

DAVID: It's supposed to be a secret but everyone will know soon enough.

JANE: Well look, why don't you come round on Sunday for lunch and tell us all about it? My parents will be there but I know they'd love to see you again.

DAVID: OK, that's a lovely idea. We'll come round on Sunday ...

Oh, I saw David today. He advised a new French restaurant in town "Le Pain" and he offer to look after our children for we can to go this restaurant with my parents, on Saturday night. Beside he remind me that your wife had been applying for a job with the BBC and says me that she had got it and had got a new computer.

Sentence structure

WORD ORDER

72 Direct object and indirect object

REMEMBER!

Some verbs can be followed by two objects: a direct object and an indirect object.

We can use:
- Verb + direct object + *to* or *for* + indirect object:
  I've lent my book to Michael.
- Verb + indirect object without *to* or *for* + direct object:
  I've lent Michael my book.

Check

Rewrite these sentences, putting the words into the correct order.

1 him money have the all I paid.

I have paid him the all money

2 lovely brought flowers me of he a bunch.

He brought me a lovely bunch of flowers

3 present grandmother have I your for a hope you bought.

I hope you have bought a present for your grandmother

4 some money give shoes the new can for me you.

Can you give me some money for the new shoes?

5 fruit you mother like this your take to I'd to.

I'd like you to take this fruit to your mother

6 give hoping job will new they am a me I.

I am hoping they will give me a new job

7 timetable please find Rose train can for the you.

Can you find the train timetable for Rose, please?

8 Andrew gave to your letter I.

I gave your letter to Andrew

9 the show why garden her you don't.

Why don't you show her the garden?

10 a everybody make for will drink I.

I will make a drink everybody

73   Order of adverbs

- An adverb describes *how, where* or *when* an action is done:
  a) *She hit him* **gently**.

- The adverb can be one word (e.g. **gently**) or a group of words – also called an adverbial phrase:
  b) *She hit him* **with all her strength**.

- Both the adverb and the adverbial phrase in these two sentences answer the question *How did she hit him?*
  Answer: a) gently. b) with all her strength.

- Adverbs that answer the question **how**? are adverbs of manner.

- Adverbs that answer the question **where**? are adverbs of place.
  They work **here**.
  I saw them **at the end of the street**.

- Adverbs that answer the question **when**? are adverbs of time.
  He left **yesterday**.
  I saw him **at four o'clock**.

- Order of adverbs:
  a) Adverbs of manner, place and time usually follow the direct object.
     I took the money **quietly**.
  b) If there is no direct object, the adverbs usually follow the verb:
     We left **at ten o'clock**.
  c) If there is more than one adverb, they are usually written:
     1 manner   2 place   3 time

	manner	*place*	*time*
I worked	hard	at the office	today.
I worked hard at the office today.			
They ran	quickly	into the house.	
They ran quickly into the house.			
We went		into the garden	at three o'clock.
We went into the garden at three o'clock.			
They played	noisily		all afternoon.
They played noisily all afternoon.			

Note: Adverbs of time and place are sometimes found at the beginning of sentences. (This emphasizes the importance of the time or place.)
Yesterday we had a really good time.
In Paris, we stayed in hotels all the time.

Practice

Rewrite these sentences in the correct order.

1 We had / at the party / a good time / yesterday.

We had a good time at the party yesterday.

2 She played / last week / at the stadium / very well.

She played very well at the stadium last week.

3 The children / in the garden / quietly / played / this afternoon.

the children played quietly in the garden this afternoon

4 He drove / through the town / very quickly.

He drove very quickly through the town

5 He sat / all through the afternoon / in his chair / quietly.

He sat quietly in his chair all through the afternoon

6 They waited / in the rain / for two or three hours / patiently.

They waited patiently in the rain for two or three hours

7 The plane / for about thirty minutes / slowly / flew / around Heathrow airport.

The plane flew slowly around Heathrow airport for about thirty minutes

8 We searched / thoroughly / the field / for several hours.

We searched the field thoroughly for several hours

9 We worked / on Sunday / in the studio / hard.

We worked hard in the studio on Sunday

10 I walked / after getting the news / slowly / to the end of the road.

I walked slowly to the end of the road after getting the news

11 He was sitting / on the edge of the bed / when I saw him / painfully.

He was sitting painfully on the edge of the bed when I saw him

12 They were arguing / in the kitchen / when I left / furiously.

They were arguing furiously in the kitchen when I left

74 Frequency adverbs

- The main frequency adverbs are:

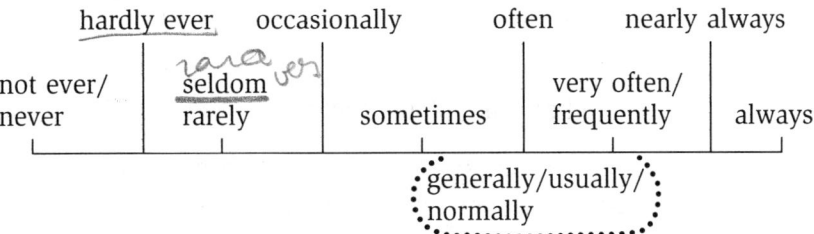

- the adverb goes between the subject and the verb:
  He **always** left the office at five o'clock.
  We **sometimes** saw them in the morning.
  I **often** have an egg for breakfast.

- If the tense uses an auxiliary verb (**will**, **have**, **be**, or **do**), the adverb comes after the auxiliary, but before the infinitive or participle.
  I'll **never** forget him.
  I've **frequently** seen him in here.
  I don't **always** agree with him.
  Do you **often** come here?

- **occasionally**, **sometimes**, **often**, **frequently**, **normally** and **generally** can follow the verb or the verb + direct object. They can also be at the beginning or end of a clause:
  I've seen him **frequently** in here.
  I've seen him in here **frequently**.
  Frequently, I've seen him in here.

Practice

Write the word given in the correct place in these sentences. Sometimes there is more than one answer. Choose the most likely one.

1 They got to the office on time. (never)

  They never got to the office on time.

2 I've seen them in the park. (sometimes)

  I've sometimes seen them in the park.

  I've seen them sometimes in the park.

3 I talked to them. (occasionally)

  Occasionally I talked to them.

4 I phoned him at the office. (occasionally)

  I phoned him occasionally at the office.

5 We'll see them again. (never)

  We'll never see them again.

6   I had written to them about their children. (frequently)

Frequently I had written to them about their children

7   Do you watch this programme? (often)

Do you watch this programme often?

8   I've been in a plane. (never)

I've never been in a plane

9   She asked how you were. (often)

She asked how you were often

10 I've complained, but it didn't change anything. (frequently)

Frequently I've complained, but it didn't change anything

11 Don't you hear from your brother now? (ever)

Don't you ever hear from your brother now?

12 I'll remember what he said. (always)

I'll always remember what he said

13 I've seen him in the supermarket. (occasionally)

Occasionally I've seen him in the supermarket

14 We agreed that we would meet again. (never)

We agreed that we would never meet again

15 I've spoken to them. (hardly ever)

I've hardly ever spoken to them

16 We saw them in the evenings. (seldom)

We saw them seldom in the evenings

17 We've sent each other cards at Christmas. (always)

We've always sent each other cards at Christmas

18 They've been waiting when I come home from work. (often)

They've often been waiting when I come home from work

19 Those children are playing football in the street. (always)

Those children are always playing football in the street

20 He's been working when I've seen him. (always)

He's always been working when I've seen him

75 Order of adjectives

There is a general order for adjectives.

number	general adj.	size	shape	age	colour	pattern	material	nationality	adjectivial noun	noun
A/An Some The Four	nice	large	square	old new	green	striped	woolen wooden metal	English Spanish French	kitchen garden	towel(s) table(s) chair(s)

For reasons of style, three or four adjectives are usually the maximum to be grouped together. When this happens, they generally follow the order in the grid.
A large old wooden table.
Four green metal garden chairs.

Practice

Write these sentences in the correct order.

1 We bought some glasses German old lovely.

   We bought some lovely old German glasses.

2 Have you seen his sports Italian car new nice?

   ....

3 He lived in a wooden old hut dirty.

   ....

4 She was wearing a beautiful shirt silk black and white.

   ....

   ....

5 Its just custom strange another country old.

   ....

6 We stood under statue an wooden old enormous.

....

....

7 They gave him clock a silver beautiful.

....

8 I bought tablecloth a large striped red and white.

....

....

9 It was old lovely scarf a woollen green.

....

10 They sent him plates blue and white china expensive very some.

....

....

76 Link words: *although, however, though, in spite of, whereas*

Practice

Rewrite the sentences, using the words given. You may need to change some words (and be careful with the punctuation). Where two answers are possible, choose the more likely one.

1 He seemed a friendly person, but I didn't like him. (although)

Although he seemed a friendly person, I didn't like him.

2 My car wouldn't start. Jenny's started immediately. (whereas)

My car wouldn't start, whereas Jenny's started immediately.

3 Jo never helped with the housework. Pat did. (whereas)

....

....

4 He lived in Germany for ten years, but he never learned German. (in spite of)

....

....

5 We sometimes stayed out late. We always got home before twelve. (though)

....

....

6 He didn't like sport: he didn't mind watching the football. (however)

....

....

7 I was very hungry. I had eaten an hour earlier. (in spite of)

....

....

8 The flat was comfortable. It was very expensive. (although)

....

....

9 My parents were angry. They soon forgave me. (though)

....

....

10 The old house was near the sea. The new one is in the middle of the town. (whereas)

....

....

QUESTIONS AND ANSWERS

77 *who* questions

What is the difference between
a) *Who saw you?* and b) *Who did you see?*

- In sentence a), **who** is the subject of the sentence:

  s   v   o   s   v   o
  Someone saw you. Who saw you?

- In sentence b), **who** is the object of the sentence:

  s   v   o   o   aux s   v
  You saw someone. Who did you see?

Notes

- **whom** can be used as the object of the sentence:
  Whom *did you see?*
  but **whom** is not used very often now.

- **what** can also be the subject of a sentence:
  What *happened?* **What** *fell off the roof?*

Practice

Make **who** questions from these sentences.

1 You were talking to someone.
   Who <u>were you talking to?</u>

2 Someone was talking to you.
   Who <u>was talking to you?</u>

3 Someone telephoned me.
   Who ....

4 They wanted to see someone.
   Who ....

5 Someone sold you the car.
   Who ....

6 Someone gave you this money.
   Who ....

7 You told someone about the contract.
   Who ....

8 They have invited some people to the party.
   Who ....

9 They were arguing with someone.
   Who ....

10 Someone complained to the manager.
   Who ....

11 Someone wrote a letter to the school.
   Who ....

12 You didn't like somebody.
   Who ....

13 Someone opened the window.
   Who ....

14 She asked someone to help.
   Who ....

15 Someone wasn't at the meeting.
   Who ....

78   Tag questions

FORM

- A tag question is formed by auxiliary + subject:
  did she? aren't they? have you?

- Positive sentences are generally followed by a negative tag question:
  *They went home, **didn't they**?   It's hot, **isn't it**?*

- Negative sentences are generally followed by a positive tag question:
  *He's not waiting for us, **is he**?   They didn't go home, **did they**?*

Notes

- Note the irregular form of ***I am*** when it is a negative tag question:
  *I'm going with you, **aren't I**?*

- Always use pronouns in tag questions:
  *Jane's your friend, isn't **she**? NOT Jane's your friend, ~~isn't Jane~~?*

USE

- Tag questions are often used to open conversations:
  It's a lovely day, isn't it?
  It's not very warm here, is it?

- They are used when we are expecting the person being questioned to agree with us:
  You're coming too, aren't you? Yes, we are.
  They're not staying much longer, are they? No, they aren't.

Practice

Rewrite these statements with tag questions.

1   It's cold.

　　It's cold, isn't it?

2   He isn't very friendly.

　　He isn't very friendly, is he?

3   You don't like eggs.

　　...

4   I'm staying too.

　　...

5   They're policemen.

　　...

6   She didn't arrive yesterday.

　　...

7   This shop's very expensive.

　　...

8 She's gone home.

   ....

9 This water's hot.

   ....

10 They're not coming this afternoon.

   ....

11 You haven't met my sister Jean.

   ....

12 He wasn't waiting at home for me.

   ....

13 She didn't like Pat when she met her.

   ....

14 They're going to write to us after they move.

   ....

15 He's got no money at the moment.

   ....

16 You liked some of the music you heard today.

   ....

17 You've nearly finished your book.

   ....

18 You're always forgetting your keys.

   ....

19 They've nearly finished the new school.

   ....

20 She's not very happy in her new job.

   ....

79 Agreeing with tag questions

- The short answer to a positive statement / negative tag is:
  Q: *He's leaving soon, isn't he?*
  A: *Yes, he is.* (agreeing with the statement)
  or: *No, he isn't.* (disagreeing with the statement)

- The short answer to a negative statement / positive tag is:
  Q: *He isn't leaving today, is he?*
  A: *No, he isn't.* (agreeing with the statement)
  or: *Yes, he is.* (disagreeing with the statement)

➤ Exercise 79 for the form of different short answers.

Practice

Write the correct short answers to agree with these questions.

1 'You're not angry, are you?'

   'No, I'm not.'

2 'They're staying in a hotel, aren't they?'

   'Yes, they are.'

3 'You said goodbye, didn't you?'

   ....

4 'She hasn't had a cup of tea, has she?'

   ....

5 'They didn't invite John, did they?'

   ....

6 'You haven't brought your car, have you?'

   ....

7 'She's seen this film already, hasn't she?'

   ....

8 'Mary isn't ill, is she?'

   ....

9 'You've heard about the meeting, haven't you?'

   ....

10 'Peter's not coming tonight, is he?'

   ....

80 Short answers

- Short answers use the auxiliary, and not the main verb. The answer to:
  Did he say that? is
  Yes, he did. (NOT ~~Yes, he said.~~)

FORM

Yes/No + subject + auxiliary verb (positive or negative)

Will you be late?	→ Yes, I will.
Has he been waiting long?	→ Yes, he has.
Do you agree?	→ Yes, I do.
Is there anything wrong?	→ No, there isn't.
Are your parents coming?	→ No, they aren't.

Note: Agreement to a negative question is indicated by using *No* and repeating the negative:
Isn't he coming ? → *No, he isn't.* (➤ Exercise 78)

Practice

Write short answers for these questions, using the positive or negative as given.

1	'You won't be late today, will you?'	'No, *I won't.*'
2	'Did they leave early this morning?'	'Yes, *they did.*'
3	'Have you checked the car?'	'Yes, ...'
4	'Is there any petrol in it?'	'Yes, ...'
5	'Have you been working here long?'	'Yes, ...'
6	'Have you finished your homework yet?'	'No, ...'
7	'Were they angry about what you said?'	'No, ...'
8	'Are they going to see us before they leave?'	'No, ...'
9	'Is he washing the dishes?'	'Yes, ...'
10	'Will you be seeing Jayne tomorrow?'	'No, ...'
11	'Haven't they told you what to do?'	'No, ...'
12	'He isn't going to apologize, is he?'	'No, ...'
13	'They haven't given you any money, have they?'	'No, ...'
14	'Hadn't she told you about Mrs Jameson?'	'No, ...'
15	'This dress is very expensive, isn't it?'	'Yes, ...'
16	'You don't like his parents, do you?'	'No, ...'
17	'He said you were wrong, didn't he?'	'Yes, ...'
18	'You won't forget the meeting, will you?'	'No, ...'
19	'It's Saturday today, isn't it?'	'Yes, ...'
20	'Didn't I talk to you about this yesterday?'	'No, ...'

81 Embedded questions

- Embedded questions are those that are 'hidden' in long questions:
  Where's the bank? (normal question)
  *Could you tell me **where the bank is**?* (embedded question)

- There are two types of embedded question:
  a) in reported speech:
     She asked me where the airport was. (➤ Exercises 64 to 66)
  b) in polite question forms, when the direct question is thought to be a little rude, and a longer question form is used:
     Could you tell me what time it is, please?
     Do you think this train is going to be late?

FORM

- The position of subject and auxiliary verb in the normal question form is reversed:

  *Where **has she** gone?* → *where **she has** gone.*

- A polite question form is now put in front of this new structure.
  Could you tell me where she has gone?

- The most commonly used polite question forms are:

Could you tell me Do you know Do you think you could tell me	if whether where how why	something	happened? has happened? will happen? is going to happen? etc.

Do you think	(that) something	happened? will happen? etc.

Note: Remember you must say: *Could you tell me where she has gone?*
(NOT ~~Could you tell me where has she gone?~~)

Practice

Write these sentences in full, using the words given.

1 Could you tell me / When does the train leave?

Could you tell me when the train leaves?

2 Do you think that / Is it going to rain today?

Do you think that it's going to rain today?

3 Do you know if / Has everybody left already?

....

4 Do you think you could tell me / What time is it, please?

....

....

5 Do you know / Why is there nobody here?

....

6 Could you tell me / Why did you leave so early?

....

7 Do you know if / Is the meeting cancelled?

....

8 Do you think / Will there be a lot of people at the party?

....

....

9 Could you tell me / What time does this shop close?

....

10 Do you know / How much is this?

....

11 Do you think you could tell me / When does the plane from Paris arrive?

....

....

12 Do you think / Will there be another train tonight?

....

13 Could you tell me / When will you be finished?

....

14 Do you know / How long will we have to wait?

....

15 Do you think you could tell me / Where's the post office?

....

....

82 *think, hope, expect, suppose*

- These verbs are often used as answers to embedded questions (and to ordinary questions, too):

'*Do you think the train will arrive soon?*'

'*Yes, I think so.*
(NOT ~~*Yes, I think.*~~)

'*I hope so.*'

'*I expect so.*' → Supongo que sí.

FORM

Positive: I think / hope / expect / suppose so.
Negative: I don't think / expect / suppose so.
I hope not.

Note: These constructions can also be used with other persons (*you, he, she, they*):
She hopes so.
They don't think so.
Do you think so?

However, the first person (*I/we*) is more commonly heard.

De cualquier manera.

Practice

Write the short answers according to the words given.

1 'Do you think we'll get there before dark?' (Yes / think)

'*Yes, I think so.*'

2 'Will there be something to eat when we get there?' (No / suppose)

'*No, I don't suppose so.*'

3 'Will the game start at three?' (Yes / expect)

Yes, I expect so

4 'Do you think we'll lose the election?' (No / suppose)

No, I don't suppose so

5 'Do you think they'll be delayed?' (No / hope)

No I hope not

6 'Do you think it'll rain tomorrow?' (No / think)

I don't think so

7 'Are the tickets going to be expensive?' (No / hope)

No I hope not

8 'Will they give Sheila a job?' (Yes / expect)

Yes, I expect so

9 'Do you think it'll be a good party?' (Yes / think)

Yes, I think so

10 'Are they going to bring the sandwiches?' (Yes / suppose)

Yes, I suppose so

RELATIVE CLAUSES

Defining relative clauses

REMEMBER!

The woman who got the job has never worked in advertising before.
The letter that arrived this morning was wrongly addressed.

- The defining relative clauses tell us which woman we are talking about and which letter we are talking about.

- Defining relative clauses are often indicated by **who** for people and **that** for things.

83 Subject and object defining relative clauses

- The noun which is being described by a clause can be either the subject or object of the relative clause:

  The man who normally works here is ill.
  Main sentence: *The man is ill.*
  Clause: *who normally works here.*

  = *he normally works here.*

  he is the subject, so this a subject relative clause.

  The man who you saw yesterday is ill.
  Main sentence: *The man is ill.*
  Clause: *who you saw yesterday.*

  = *you saw him yesterday.*

  him is the object, so this is an object relative clause.

Practice

Underline each relative clauses and write S or O to indicate whether it is a subject or object clause.

1 The woman who I spoke to wasn't very polite. *O*
2 The machine that worked better than the others cost the least. *S*
3 I wouldn't stay in a hotel that refused to accept children. *S*
4 I don't understand people who hate animals. *S*
5 The stereo that I bought last week doesn't work properly. *O*
6 The television that they have designed is going to be very expensive. *O*
7 That man who complained is always making trouble. *S*
8 The woman who gave us all this money is not very rich. *S*
9 I admire people who can speak more than one language. *S*
10 The assistant who you complained about has been moved. *O*

84 Contact clauses (relative clauses without *who, that,* or *which*)

- If a clause is an object relative clause and it is defining (➤ Exercise 85), *who*, *that*, or *which* is not necessary:
  a) *She's the person who I met at the conference.*
     → *She's the person I met at the conference.*
  b) *Have you seen the dress that I've just bought?*
     → *Have you seen the dress I've just bought?*

Note: This is not possible with subject relative clauses:
The man who was feeling ill left early.
(NOT ~~The man was feeling ill left early~~.)

Practice

Write each pair of sentences as one, without using **who**, **that**, or **which**. Think carefully about the word order.

1 I shouted at a man. He didn't come back again.

The man I shouted at didn't come back again. [who]

2 I dropped a television. It never worked again.

The television I dropped never worked again. [that]

3 I hired a machine. It was broken. [alquila]

..A machine I hired was broken..............................

4 She bought some clothes. They were beautiful.

..the clothes She bought were beautiful..

5 They built a wall. It fell down after three weeks.

..The wall they built fell down after three weeks.

6 I asked a policeman. He wasn't very helpful.

..The policeman I asked wasn't very helpful..

7 We bought a car. I didn't really like it.

..I didn't really like the car we bought..

8 I borrowed some money from Janice. I lost it.

..I lost the money I borrowed some money

9 They sent a new teacher. I really liked her.

..I really liked a new teacher they sent

10 I sacked a sales assistant. I had a terrible argument with him.

..I had a terrible argument with the sales assistant I sacked.

85 *whose*

- **whose** is used to indicate possession:
  There's the man. His wallet was stolen.
  → *There's the man whose wallet was stolen.*

Note the difference between **whose** and **who's**: who's is never used to indicate possession, but is a contraction of **who is** or **who has**:
  She's the one who's lending us the money. (who's lending = who is lending)

Practice

Express each pair of sentences as one, using *whose* or *who's*.

1 There's the lady. Her dog was killed.

There's the lady whose dog was killed.

2 That's the man. He's going to buy the company.

That's the man who's going to buy the company.

3 He's the person. His car was stolen.

He's the person whose car was stolen.

4 She's the new doctor. She's coming to the hospital next month.

She's the new doctor who's coming to the hospital next month

5 She's the journalist. Her article was on the front page of *The Times*.

She's the journalist whose article was on the front page of The Times.

6 They're the people. Their shop burned down last week.

They're the people whose shop burned down last week.

7 That's the sales director. He's leaving in March.

That's the sales director who's leaving in March.

8 That's the student. Her parents complained about the school.

that's the student whose parents complained about the school.

9 She's the singer. She's just signed a contract with a recording company.

She's the singer who's just signed a contract with a recording company.

10 He's the person. He's going to be promoted.

He's the person who's going to be promoted.

11 I'm the one. My flat was broken into.

I'm the one whose flat was broken into

12 She's the person. She's working for the film studios.

She's the person who's working for the film studios.

13 That's the architect. She's just won a prize for design.

....

....

14 That's the boy. He's just got a place at university.

....

....

15 I'm the person. You stayed in my flat.

....

86   Defining and non-defining relative clauses: recognition

* There are two types of relative clause: defining and non-defining.

* Defining clauses are more common than non-defining clauses:
  'I saw that man again.'
  'Which man?'
  'The man who wants to buy my house.'
  who wants to buy my house is an example of a defining clause: it defines
  (= explains) exactly who or what is being discussed. It can also be used in a
  longer sentence:
  The man who wants to buy my house is coming to see me.
  I saw the man who wants to buy my house again.

* Non-defining clauses give information about the subject being discussed, but it
  is not essential information:
  A man, who said he knew my father, asked me for money.
  who said he knew my father is an interesting fact but it is extra rather than
  essential information. Non-defining clauses are indicated by the use of
  commas before and after the clause.

Notes

* Non-defining clauses are used in writing but are not used frequently in conversation, where
  two short sentences can be enough:
  I'm going to see Sheila, who I told you about yesterday.
  I'm going to see Sheila. I told you about her yesterday.

* The difference between defining (D) and non-defining (ND) clauses is important because:
  a) they can change the meaning of a sentence:
  D: *I have two sisters who are living in New York at the moment.*
  ND: *I have two sisters, who are living in New York at the moment.*
  In the defining sentence, the person has two sisters in New York and may have more
  sisters somewhere else.
  In the non-defining sentence, the person has only two sisters.

  b) Different relative pronouns (**who, that, which**, etc.) are used for defining and non-
  defining clauses (➤ Exercise 86).

Practice

Write D or ND to indicate whether the clause is defining or non-defining.

1 The bus, which arrived late, was full. *ND*
2 The bus which they sent didn't have enough seats. *D*
3 The house which we wanted to buy was too expensive.
4 The house, which we wanted to buy, was too expensive.
5 I have two brothers who are working as architects at the moment.
6 I have two brothers, who are working as architects at the moment.
7 I never met the doctor, who lived next door for five years.
8 Did I ever tell you about my uncle, who left school when he was 15?
9 I didn't agree with the man who said we should cancel the trip.
10 She's one of those people who will argue about anything.

87   Relative pronouns in defining and non-defining clauses

who, that, or *which*?

Defining:

	person	*thing*
Subject	who (or that)	that (or which)
Object	– (or that)	– (or that)

Non-defining:

	person	*thing*
Subject	, who … ,	, which … ,
Object	, who (or whom) … ,	, which … ,

Notes

- Words in brackets ( ) are possible alternatives to the words given, but are less common.
- *whom* is used only in formal English.
- Object relative clauses do not normally need *who* or *that* (➤ Exercise 83)

Practice

Write *who, that, which,* or nothing to complete these sentences. The boxes above will help you, but do not use the words in brackets.

1 Have you got the money .–. I lent you yesterday?
2 Peter, .*who*. I had seen earlier, wasn't at the party.

3 This is the machine .**that**. cost half a million pounds.

4 Mary, **who** had been listening to the conversation, looked angry.

5 Have you read the book .... I gave you?

6 The house, **which** they bought three months ago, look lovely.

7 Mrs Jackson, .**who**. had been very ill, died yesterday.

8 Is this the person **who** *(the one)* stole your handbag?

9 The dog, .**Which** had been very quiet, suddenly started barking.

10 I didn't receive the letters .... she sent me.

11 My mother, .**who**. had been talking to them earlier, knew that they were in the building.

12 The old man, .**who**.had been injured by the flying stones, was very frightened.

14 We didn't like the secretary .... the agency sent.

15 I didn't find the money .... *(or that)* you said you'd left.

88 *which* referring to whole sentences

- *which* in relative clauses generally refers to nouns:
  He turned on the television, which looked new and expensive.
  which here refers to **the television**.

- *which* can also refer to whole sentences:
  He turned on the television. I thought this was rather surprising.
  He turned on the television, which I thought was rather surprising.

Notes

- *which* here refers to **the action of turning on the television**, not just to the television.

- *which* can be used like this only in non-defining relative clauses (➤ Exercise 85).

Practice

Express these pairs of sentences as one, using *which*.

1 I love the countryside. That is why I want to go and live there.

   I love the countryside, which is why I want to go and live there.

2 They stayed for hours. I was very annoyed about this.

   They stayed for hours, which I was very annoyed about.

3 He passed all his exams. This surprised us.

   He passed all his exams which this surprised us.

4   They forgot about my birthday. This was a bit disappointing.

They forgot about my birthday which was a bit disappointing

5   The pilot showed us how to fly the plane. It was extremely interesting.

The pilot showed us to fly the plane which was extremely interesting

6   I couldn't get a flight to Malaga. This upset the children.

I couldn't get a flight to Malaga which upset the children

7   He was rude and aggressive. His behaviour made me very angry.

He was rude and aggressive which behaviour made me very angry

8   They said they couldn't pay for the car immediately. This made me a bit suspicious.

They said they couldn't pay for the car immediately which made me a bit

9   The policeman asked me for directions. This confused me a little.

The policeman asked me for directions which confused me a little

10 The restaurant wouldn't accept cheques. I found this rather surprising.

The restaurant wouldn't accept cheques which I found this rather surprising

89   *where, when,* and *why* in relative clauses

- *where* and *when* can be used to introduce defining and non-defining relative clauses:
  We visited the town where I was born. (defining)
  I bought them at the supermarket, where I met Mrs Butler. (non-defining)
  I saw the film last year, when I was in Paris. (non-defining)
  I think that was the time when I lost all my money. (defining)

- Less often, *why* can also be used to introduce a defining clause: it usually follows *a reason* or *the reason*:
  There must be a reason why you said that.

Practice

Write **where**, **when**, or **why** to complete these sentences.

1 We visited the school ...*where*... my father taught.

2 I met her last month, ...*when*... she came to our house.

3 We all looked at the place ...*where*... the fire had started.

4 I met him in the café, ...*when*... he was working as a waiter.

5 Do you remember the time ...*when*... Adrian fell off his bicycle?

6 Did they tell you the reason ...*why*... they were late?

7 The cat sat on the wall, ...*where*... it had a good view of the birds.

8 I'm talking about the time ...*why*... they didn't have cars.

9 Last year I spent my holiday in Spain, ...*where*... I met Andy.

10 I couldn't understand the reason ...*why*... they were so rude.

11 I bought them last year, ...*when*... I was in France.

12 We went away in August, ...*when*... the children were on holiday from school.

13 I never liked the house ...*where*... my husband was born.

14 They arrived in the evening, at a time ...*when*... we were all out.

15 I listen to music late at night, ...*when*... the children have gone to bed.

Prepositions and phrasal verbs

PREPOSITIONS

90 Prepositions

> **REMEMBER!**
>
> Prepositions can be used to indicate position, movement and time.

Check

Complete the sentences, using a preposition from the box.

on	at	in	out of	off	through
round	down	under	over		

1 This picture keeps falling ......*off*...... the wall.

2 I'm tired. I've been walking ...*round*... the shops all morning.

3 James is ......*at*......... college now.

4 There's no gate so we'll have to climb ....*over*..... the fence.

5 There's a stain .....*on*........ my new shirt.

6 Can you see my keys ....*in*....... that drawer?

7 Be careful with that case. You might fall ...*down*... the steps.

8 Can you help me get my bags ...*out of*... the car?

9 I can't get this table ...*through*... the door.

10 That boat's too tall to go ...*under*... the bridge.

91 Prepositions used in idioms

- Prepositions are sometimes used idiomatically:

I got the job **through** my uncle.

*I got the job **through** my uncle.*

*She's been promoted. She's got two hundred people working **under** her now.*

Practice

Use these prepositions to complete the sentences.

in front of	against	below
behind	against	below
behind	between	above
past	on top of	above

1 He doesn't do much work in the house: in fact, he seems to think he's
...*above*... that sort of thing.

2 It's a very good article. There's obviously a lot of research ...behind... it.

3 I work for an organization which campaigns ...against... smoking.

4 It was very cold, about twenty degrees ...below... zero.

5 He tells me everything. There are no secrets ...between... us.

6 It was difficult to get the idea ...past... the board of directors, but they
finally agreed.

7 The company is doing well; sales were ...above... average last month.

8 I think you should forget about your argument and put it all ...behind...
you.

9 They have a very good future ...in front of... them.

10 It's terrible: their wages are ...below... the national minimum.

11 We've never played ...against... a Swiss team before.

12 The work was difficult at first, but I soon got ...on top of... it.

PHRASAL VERBS

REMEMBER!

Phrasal verbs are formed with a verb + preposition or a verb + adverb:

We need to set off early tomorrow.
Did you find out the times of the trains?
I requested a pay rise but they turned me down.

- A phrasal verb is formed when a preposition (**up**, **down**, **in**, etc.) or an adverb
(**away**, **back**, etc.) is added to a verb to produce a new verb with a different
meaning:

*I **get up** at eight o'clock.*

*We'll **pick** you **up** outside the station.*

*The plane **took off** very quickly.*

- The meaning of a phrasal verb can be similar to the original verb:
  *The car **slowed down** and then stopped.* (= similar meaning to **slow**)
  – or it can be completely different from the original:
  *I'm going to **give up** smoking.* (= different meaning from **give**)

- There are four main types of phrasal verb which are described in Exercises 91 to 94.

92   Some common phrasal verbs

blow up	~~grow up~~	put off	look after
break down	keep on	run out of	give up
find out	let down	set off	wake up
get over	look out	tell off	stand up
go on	look up	turn down	sit down

Practice

Write the above verbs in the correct tenses to complete these sentences. Use each verb once only.

1   We'll buy a smaller house when the children have .*grown up*. and left home.

2   Who's going to .... the cats when we go away on holiday?

3   'Sorry, we .... flour,' she said. 'We'll have some next week.'

4   The computer isn't working – it .... this morning.

5   It was really difficult to .... this morning after my late night last night.

6   I .... where he lived by checking in the local library.

7   It was no problem: we .... his number in the telephone book.

8   Everyone in court had to .... when the judge arrived.

9   They .... working all through the night, and finished at nine this morning.

10 'I can't come today,' he said. 'We'll have to .... the meeting until next week.'

11 We must .... early on Sunday morning to avoid the traffic.

12 I was .... by the teacher because I hadn't done my homework.

13 My headaches have been much better since I .... drinking coffee.

14 He had a very painful illness, but he's .... it now.

15 'What's .... here? What are you doing?

16 '........................!' she cried. 'He's got a gun!'

17 I .... their offer because they weren't going to pay me enough money.

18 Can't you do the washing up? You .... all day and I'm exhausted.

19 He promised to play in the match, but he didn't come. He .... the whole team.

20 The car burned for a few minutes, then the petrol tank .... with a loud bang.

93 Phrasal verbs that do not take an object

- Some phrasal verbs do not take an object:
  *The plan **fell through**: we had to cancel the project.*

get by	~~pass away~~	sleep in
grow up	set off	take off

Practice

Put the above verbs into the correct sentences, using the right tense.

1 She had a terrible shock when her father *passed away*.

2 I didn't have to go to work that morning, so I decided to ....

3 How do you .... with so little money?

4 The explorers .... in the morning, before it was too hot.

5 After the children .... and left, the house seemed empty.

6 What time does the plane ....?

94 Separable phrasal verbs that take an object

- We can say:
  *We **picked up** the children at three.* or
  *We **picked** the children **up** at three.*

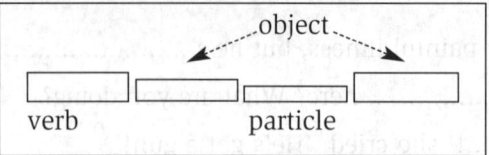

- the direct object can go:
  a) **before** the particle (= preposition or adverb)
     *We decided to **cut** the tree **down**.*
  b) **after** the particle:
     *We decided to **cut down** the tree.*

- If the object is a pronoun (**him**, **me**, **it**, etc.) it goes **before** the particle:
  *We decided to **cut** it **down**.*
  (NOT ~~We cut down it~~.)

Practice

Write these sentences, putting the verbs and objects in the correct order. Where two answers are possible, write them both.

1 How do you / slow down / the machine?

How do you slow down the machine?

How do you slow the machine down?

2 The company decided to / give away / a hundred pounds.

....

....

3 I / turned on / the television.

....

....

4 It's a nice dress: would you like to / try on / it?

....

....

5   the government wants to / close down / the factory.

   ....

   ....

6   It's too wet for football. I think we'll have to / call off / it.

   ....

   ....

7   I couldn't accept his offer so I / turned down / him.

   ....

   ....

8   The baby's fallen over: would you / pick up / her?

   ....

   ....

95   Phrasal verbs that take an object but do not separate

- This type of verb is a unit that is not split by the object:
  How are we going to get round this problem?
  (NOT *How are we going to get this problem round?*)

verb   particle   object

The object must follow the particle.

Practice

Write these sentences, putting the verbs and objects in the correct order.

1   She looks like her mother: don't you think she / her / after / takes?

   She looks like her mother: don't you think she takes after her?

2   His wife died. He / her death / over / got / never.

   ....

   ....

3   She has a small pension. She / off / lives / that.

   ....

   ....

Prepositions and phrasal verbs

4 When Pat and John visited their parents, / the children / after / I / looked.

  ....

  ....

5 I'm sorry, I forgot your sunglasses: you'll have to / them / without / do.

  ....

  ....

6 I saw Peter today. He / you / after / asked.

  ....

  ....

96 Phrasal verbs with two particles

- This type of phrasal verb is a unit that does not split:
  'I'm not going to put up with this,' he said.

verb	particle	particle	object

The object follows the second particle.

ran out of	keep on at	look down on
come up with	go back on	

Practice

Choose one of the above verbs to complete each sentence below.

1 I'm afraid we've *ran out of* milk.

2 He doesn't like them: I think he .... people who haven't got any money.

3 You can trust her: she never *go back on* her promises.

4 He .... me until I agreed to go to the party with him.

5 She *came up with* an idea that solved the problem.

occurred

134

97   Summary of phrasal verbs

	Type	Example
1	verb takes no object	The plane **takes off** at ten.
2	verb takes object: verb can split	I **looked up** the word in the dictionary. I **looked** the word **up** in the dictionary. I **looked** it **up** in the dictionary.
3	verb takes object: verb cannot split	I saw John today: he **asked after** you.
4	verb has two particles: does not split	We've **run out of** bread.

Notes

- Many verbs are followed by prepositions, but this does not mean that they are phrasal verbs. A phrasal verb has a meaning as a unit. The following are verbs + prepositions:

  *What do you **think about** the idea?*
  ***Look at** these clothes!*

  With verbs + prepositions, the direct object always follows the preposition, but the preposition does not have to come immediately after the verb:

  *We **looked** carefully **at** all the clothes.*
  *He **thought** for some minutes, and with much regret, **about** his parents.*

- Phrasal verbs can sometimes be type 1, or type 2, depending on their meaning:

  *'Goodbye!' she said, and **hung up**. (= put the phone down). (type 1)*
  *I ˌhung my coat **up** behind the door. (type 2)*

- If the object (o) contains a large number of words, then the type 2 phrasal verb does not split:

  *Have you **looked up** |ᵒ the word were talking about this morning?*

98   Deducing phrasal verbs from context

- Sometimes the meaning of a phrasal verb can be understood from the context of the sentence:
  *It will hurt at first, but the pain will soon **wear off**.*
  It is not difficult to guess that ***wear off*** means 'to get less and less until it disappears'.

Practice

98a Read this passage and think about the meanings of the missing verbs. Do not write them in yet.

'... I was having a terrible time until recently. About a month ago I was feeling really fed up with my job: nothing was going right, and I hated going to work. My boss was always (1) *getting at* me – ordering me around and telling me I hadn't done things properly: I just couldn't

(2)..*put up with* it any longer. I'd even (3)...*go off*........ the work itself: I used to like it, but I wasn't getting any enjoyment out of it any more. Then one day the boss came in and accused me of (4)..*drift in*..... late for work all the time. I couldn't believe it! I'd only been late once that month and he was always (5)..*drift in*.. halfway through the morning. I asked him where he'd (6)..*got hold of*. this information and he said that one of the secretaries had told him. I said that it just wasn't true and that she must be (7)....*pick up on*. me because she didn't like me. Anyway, I got really annoyed and in the end just (8)....*storm out*, slamming the door behind me. I (9)...*hand in*.... my resignation and left that day.

Well, fortunately things have (10)..*pick up*..... since then. I (11)...*take up*..... evening classes in photography after leaving my job and met a solicitor there. She (12)*comes up with* the idea that I should go and work in her office, so I did! It's much more interesting than the last job so, as it happened, things (13)..*work out*.... well in the end!

98b Here is a list of verbs with their definitions. Choose the correct phrasal verbs and write them in the correct tenses to complete the passage above.

~~get at~~ – continually annoy	hand in – give (resignation, or an official form) to an office
come up with – suggest	
work out – eventually develop	put up with – tolerate
get hold of – obtain	pick up – improve
storm out – leave angrily	go off – not like any more
pick on – choose for unpleasant treatment	take up – start
	turn up – arrive
	drift in (colloquial) – arrive lazily

Test 1

Part A

Circle the correct words.

1 The (*dog's*/*dogs'*) heads were very dirty.

2 I've seen the (*children's*/*childrens'*) school.

3 Where are (*the girls' jackets*/*the jackets of the girls*)?

4 She quietly opened the (*laboratory's door*/*laboratory door*). ✓

5 The garden is at (*the house's front*/*the front of the house*). ✓

6 She's just had a (*week's holiday*/*week holiday*).

7 I've broken the (*kitchen door*/*kitchen's door*). ✓

8 She's the (*doctor's receptionist*/*doctor receptionist*).

9 I'm (*the manager of the London office*/*the London office's manager*).

10 It's (*six day work*/*six day's work*). ✓

SCORING

10 points. *Give yourself a point for each correct answer.* Score 9

Part B

Write **a**, **an**, **the**, or **–** for no article.

1 I'm sorry, Mrs Evans has gone ....–........ home. ✓

2 It's a fast car – it can travel at 300 kilometres ...an.... hour. ✓

3 Platinum is more expensive than ....–........ gold. ✓

4 Oh good! It's ...the... postman! ✓

5 I've just bought .....a....... guitar. ✓

6 Do you enjoy playing .....the.. piano? ✓

7 Take these pills three times ....a...... day. ✓

8 Do you think ....–........ French is a difficult language? ✓

9 ..the.... moon is very beautiful tonight. ✓

10 Have you washed ......a...... dishes?
the

SCORING

10 points. *Give yourself a point for each correct answer.* Score 9

Part C

Write the correct form of the comparative or superlative.

✓ 1 This is ...the highest... mountain in the country. (high)

✓ 2 She's only twelve, but she's ...taller than... her mother. (tall)

✓ 3 He's just bought the most expensive... computer in the shop. (expensive)

✓ 4 Pat's the most intelligent... student in the class. (intelligent)

✓ 5 My uncle was ...shorter than... me. (short)

✓ 6 It was the ugliest... dog I have ever seen. (ugly)

✓ 7 I had the most wonderful... holiday of my life (wonderful).

✓ 8 He's ...the laziest... person I've ever met. (lazy)

9 Food is ...most expensive... here. (expensive)

✓ 10 This school is ...better than... the other one. (good)

SCORING

10 points. *Give yourself a point for each correct answer.*   Score 9

Part D

Circle the mistakes and write the correct sentences.

✓ 1 Were you frightened of the wolfs?
   Were you frightened of the wolves?

✓ 2 The ladys walked quickly out of the room.
   The ladies walked quickly out of the room

✓ 3 The room was full of shelfs.
   The room was full of shelves

✓ 4 There were a lot of persons at the party.
   There were a lot of people at the party.

✓ 5 The packed everything into boxs.
   They packed everything into boxes

✓ 6 Could I have tin of peas please?
   Could I have a tin of peas please?

138

7 A lot of people wear the fur now.

A lot of people wear fur now ✓

8 The machine's made of a silver.

The machine's made of silver ✓

9 It was the terrible experience.

It was the horrible experience

10 She's a sculptor – she works with the stone.

She's a sculptor – she works with stone ✓

SCORING

10 points. *Give yourself a point for each correct answer.*   Score 8

Part E

Write *so* or *such* to complete the sentences.

1 I was very embarrased – it was ......such...... a stupid mistake!

2 He was ....so........ ill that I took him to hospital.

3 They worked ....so........ slowly that they didn't finish!

4 It was ....so........ expensive that I didn't buy it.

5 It was ...such..... an expensive shop that I walked out.

6 Why are you always ......so............ rude?

7 Please don't make ......such.... a terrible noise!

8 It was ....such.. a nice car that I bought it.

9 You look ....so........ healthy!

10 She was ....such.. a lovely person. I'll always remember her.

SCORING

10 points. *Give yourself a point for each correct answer.*   Score 10

TOTAL SCORE

Maximum 50 points. *Add up your score.*   Total Score ☐

Test 2

Part A

Complete the letter with the correct form of the verbs.

Dear Marty

How are you? I (1) .....am......staying...... (stay) in a hotel in
Hawaii at the moment, because we (2) ....are....looking.at...
(look at) the night sky. I (3) .....know...................... (know) you
(4) ......are....having........ (have) a holiday now, because Maria
wrote to me. (5) ....Are...you...enjoing. (you enjoy?) Texas?
I (6) ....believe........ (believe) you (7) are....writting...
(visit) Glen this week - give him my love!

The sky above Hawaii is fantastic. We usually (8) ..start...................
(start) work at ten in the evening and (9) ..finish..........................
(finish) at seven the next morning. At the moment I (10) am...studying.
(study) the mountains on the moon - you (11) .know........................
(know) I (12) ...writing.................... (write) a report on the moon
for the Institute. It's nearly finished! Professor Jordan
(13) ....is...working.......... (work) in Hawaii right now – though of
course he (14) ......lives..................... (live) in new York – and he
helps a lot. He (15) ...is...sitting............... (sit) next to me as I
write, and he sends his regards!

Take care,

Pat

SCORING
15 points. *Give yourself a point for each correct answer.* Score ⊞

Part B

Write the verbs in the present perfect or the past simple.

1 I'm sorry, I ...have....broken... a glass. (break)

2 I ...have.lived...... in this street since I was a child. (live)

3 We ...had...moved.... here three years ago. (move)

4 ...Have...you been. to the USA? (you/be)

140

5 I ....*I've been*.... in this class for two years. (be)

6 She opened the door and ....*shouted*.... for help. (shout)

7 I *have never done* this before. (never do)

8 John called a minute ago. He ....*said*.... he was feeling miserable. (say)

9 I phoned her and ....*apologized*.... (apologize)

10 She ....*has stayed*.... for a while but then left. (stay)

11 She ....*had*.... a lot of jobs since she was at school. (have)

12 The rabbit stopped and ....*looked*.... at me. (look)

13 When ....*did she die*.... (she die?)

14 He ....*has just left*.... (just leave)

15 I ....*worked*.... here for fifteen years – I think I'm getting bored. (work)

SCORING

15 points. *Give yourself a point for each correct answer.*   Score 12

Part C

Circle the mistakes and write the correct sentences.

1 (Will) I carry your suitcase for you?

Shall I carry your suitcase for you?

2 Wait a minute - I will (have opened) the door.

Wait a minute. I will open the door.

3 The plane to Paris (is going to leave) at ten, stop at Amsterdam and arrive at twelve.

The plane to Paris leaves at ten, stop at Amsterdam and arrive at twelve

4 Look at those clouds. (It'll) rain.

Look at those clouds. It's going to rain.

5 I'll never (speaking) to him again.

I'll never speak to him again

6 Will she studies history at university?

✓ *Will she study history at university?*

7 Next november we're going to be married for fifteen years.

Next november we will have been married 15 yea—

8 I'm going to leave early because it was raining, but I didn't.

✗ *I was going to leave early because it was raining, but I didn't.*

9 My mother is being angry when she finds out.

My mother will be angry when she finds out

10 He's hating me if he can't come to the party.

✓ *He will hate me if he can't come to the party*

SCORING

10 points. *Give yourself a point for each correct answer.*

Score 6

Part D

Rewrite these sentences in the passive. Keep them in the same tense, and remove
they, **we**, **someone**, etc.

1 We check the aeroplanes every month.

The aeroplanes are checked every month

2 Someone has given him some new clothes.

He has been given some new clothes

3 We clean these rooms every evening.

These rooms are cleaned every evening

4 They sold two million copies of the books last year.

two million copies of the books were sold last year

5 They check the examination papers in this room.

The examination papers are checked in this room

6 As soon as you arrive in the hospital, someone checks your temperature.

Your temperature is checked

7 No one has invited him.

He hasn't been invited

8 We send the lorries by aeroplane.

the lorries are sent by aeroplane

142

9 Someone opens the gates at ten o'clock.

the gates are opened at 10 o'clock

10 Steven Spielberg directed this film.

this film was directed by Steven Spielberg

SCORING

10 points. *Give yourself a point for each correct answer.*   Score ☐

TOTAL SCORE

Maximum 50 points. *Add up your score.*   Total Score ☐

Test 3

Part A

Complete the sentences, putting the verbs into the correct tense.

1 If you'd phoned the police, you (not be) _wouldn't have been_ injured.

2 He'll come to the party if you (invite) _invite_ him.

3 I (make) _'ll make_ the tea if you make the sandwiches.

4 I'm sorry you didn't come. You (enjoy) _would have enjoyed_ it.

5 Tell me if anything strange (happen) _happens_ .

6 Why isn't Patrick here? He (have) _would have had_ a great time!

7 If someone rings the bell, (answer) _answer_ it.

8 They (be) _'ll be_ exhausted if they've been travelling all night.

9 The machine (stop) _stops_ if you turn this key.

10 If I (be) _were_ you, I wouldn't do that.

SCORING

10 points. *Give yourself a point for each correct answer.* Score ☐

Part B

Circle the correct words to complete the sentences.

1 (*Could*/Should) you turn down the radio please?.

2 You (*needn't*/mustn't) come this weekend – it's not really necessary.

3 'Do you think I (may/*should*) stay at home tonight?'

   'Yes, I do. You've gone out too much already this week.'

4 The weather report says it (*might*/can) snow this weekend.

5 (*Can*/May) you call me tonight, please?

6 I tried to move it, but I (*couldn't*/can't).

7 I (*can't*/mustn't) see you on Thursday. I've got a meeting.

8 It's not very formal, you (*don't have to*/mustn't) wear smart clothes.

9 I'm sorry, this is a quiet room. You (don't have to/*mustn't*) make a noise.

10 It was a warm night, so I (*didn't have to*/mustn't) take a coat.

SCORING

10 points. *Give yourself a point for each correct answer.* Score ☐

144

Part C

Put **could**, **must**, **should**, **shouldn't**, **might**, or **can't** in the past tense in the spaces provided.

1 Mark (take) .... the money – he's only three!

2 He (leave) .... if he'd wanted to.

3 I'm sorry, I (phone) .... when they didn't arrive.

4 We don't know who was driving. Both Mr and Mrs Cooper (drive) .... the car.

5 I'm not interested in why you were late. You (be) .... here on time.

6 John was in the room. He (hear) .... the accident.

7 Yes, I know I (stop) .... him – but I didn't.

8 It was dark and cold. The children (go out) ....

9 Alan (take) .... her purse. No one else knew it was there.

10 I (go) .... skiing if I'd wanted to.

SCORING
10 points. *Give yourself a point for each correct answer.*   Score ☐

Part D

Write these sentences as indirect speech. Change any words which need to be changed.

1 'Which coat did you take?' (He ...)

....

2 'I'll see you on Tuesday,' he said.

....

3 'How much was it?' (They ...)

....

4 'Would you hurry up, please?' she asked.

....

5 'Would you sit down, please?' he asked.

....

6 'I can't do it,' she said.

....

7 'I'll send an e-mail from the airport,' she said.

....

8 'Would you turn on the computer?' he asked.

....

9 'Why can't I connect to the Internet?' he asked.

....

10 'I'm sorry I'm late,' he said.

....

SCORING
10 points. *Give yourself a point for each correct answer.* Score ☐

Part E

Complete the short answers to these questions.

1 'Mary won't be there, will she?' 'No, ...'
2 'You didn't see her, did you?' 'Yes, ...'
3 'Your parents are coming, aren't they?' 'No, ...'
4 'You've already done your homework, haven't you?'
   'No, ...'
5 'Peter and Eric have lived here for years, haven't they?'
   'Yes, ...'
6 'You don't like me, do you?' 'No, ...'
7 'We've been waiting here for an hour, haven't we?' 'Yes,
   ....'
8 'They wouldn't want to come early, would they?' 'No, ...'

9 'It doesn't work very well, does it?' 'No, ...'

10 'She'll have seen this before, won't she?' 'Yes, ...'

SCORING

10 points. *Give yourself a point for each correct answer.*   Score ☐

TOTAL SCORE

Maximum 50 points. *Add up your score.*   Total Score ☐

Key

1 1 the piano 2 a mouth 3 the office ... gone home 4 the garden 5 French and Italian 6 warmth 7 the sun 8 the dog ... a walk 9 sugar 10 in Scotland 11 a couple of minutes 12 the piano 13 a fast car ... 150 miles an hour 14 to work 15 the front door 16 wine ... alcohol 17 a dozen eggs ... a loaf 18 a ton 19 the washing-up 20 glass 21 tea ... milk 22 the radio 23 a cup 24 a diamond necklace 25 the army

2 1 a tin 2 the tin 3 tin 4 wood 5 a wood 6 the wood 7 the paper 8 paper 9 a paper 10 a chocolate 11 chocolate 12 The chocolates 13 dress 14 The dress 15 a beautiful dress 16 the experience 17 experience 18 a wonderful experience 19 the noise 20 a strange noise 21 noise

3 I could tell by *the* town hall clock that I was late, so I decided to catch *a* bus. It was *a* beautiful day: *the* sun was shining and there was very little wind. I turned *the* corner, and walked down *the* main street. *A* couple of minutes later, I heard *a* noise, and *a* man wearing *a* grey leather jacket ran past me. At first, I thought he was trying to catch *the* bus which was waiting at *the* bus stop – but then *a* policeman appeared, running at some speed. He was obviously chasing *the* man in *the* leather jacket, and he was joined by another policeman, who was talking rapidly into *a* hand-held radio.

All three disappeared into *a* crowd of people, my bus arrived, and I got on. As *the* bus drove down *the* road, I saw *the* man again, walking casually through *the* crowd with his coat over his shoulder. I could also see *the* second policeman, still talking into his radio. He was describing *a* man who no longer existed, *a* man wearing *a* jacket and running furiously: while *the* real criminal (if he was *a* criminal) walked slowly and casually into *the* station.

4 1 boy's books 2 car door 3 pocket of my suit 4 kitchen door. 5 men's clothes 6 car boot/the boot of the car 7 front of the hotel 8 chimpanzees' behaviour 9 sitting-room carpet 10 chair leg/leg of the chair 11 week's rest 12 President's secretary 13 kitchen light 14 front of my car 15 cinema manager/manager of the cinema 16 garden wall 17 fortnight's holiday 18 bathroom window 19 three hours' delay 20 my parents' house

5 1 glasses 2 halves 3 tomatoes ... sandwiches 4 fish 5 stereos ... videos 6 potatoes 7 cats ... mice 8 houses ... roofs 9 leaves 10 handkerchiefs 11 processes ... cars 12 chickens ... sheep 13 discos 14 books ... plays 15 shelves ... glasses 16 boys ... countries 17 stories 18 worries 19 knives ... forks 20 wolves ... deer

6 1 warmer 2 most expensive 3 highest 4 bigger 5 most beautiful 6 more modern 7 oldest 8 prettier 9 more difficult 10 largest

7 1 warmer than 2 as long as 3 the worst 4 faster than 5 easier than 6 the most difficult 7 as good as 8 more sensitive than 9 quicker than 10 more expensive than 11 the best 12 more cheerful than 13 as intelligent as 14 longer than 15 as good as

8 1 such 2 so 3 so 4 such 5 such 6 so 7 such 8 so 9 so 10 such

9 1 you're reading 2 We usually go 3 She writes 4 He is/He's playing 5 My boss flies 6 I'm/I am cooking 7 That man is/man's trying 8 Do you walk 9 The bank does not/doesn't open 10 Her son does not/doesn't visit

10 1 are you thinking 2 do you think 3 I don't agree 4 Are you looking 5 Do you prefer 6 I don't like 7 I hear 8 I don't remember 9 Are you listening 10 I hate 11 I'm not looking forward 12 They're looking 13 don't you agree 14 does this mean? 15 I don't understand 16 I never agree 17 he knows 18 They're watching

11 1 I live … I'm staying 2 Sheila's using … uses 3 We usually stay … we're celebrating 4 I come … I'm living 5 I'm staying … I have 6 They usually work … they aren't working 7 He teaches … he's working 8 The business usually makes … it's doing 9 I usually work … I'm having 10 I'm studying … I don't speak

12 1 painted 2 were having 3 was playing 4 made 5 Did you see 6 was working 7 were talking 8 slept 9 destroyed 10 was waiting

13 1 looked 2 were standing 3 was passing 4 was giving/gave 5 were working/worked 6 was getting/got 7 could not 8 was emptying 9 were behaving/behaved 10 coughed 11 said 12 dropped

14 1n 2c 3g 4o 5a 6m 7k 8i 9l 10e 11h 12j 13b 14f 15d

15 1 have met 2 has travelled 3 was 4 decided 5 has changed 6 went 7 was 8 took 9 hitch-hiked 10 has visited 11 was 12 made 13 never forgot/has never forgotten 14 was 15 was 16 stole 17 lost 18 had 19 made 20 has returned 21 went 22 worked 23 has made 24 has learned 25 has had 26 has often been 27 has never thought 28 went 29 changed 30 have wanted

16 1 's been 2 have you been doing 3 haven't stopped 4 've been writing 5 answering 6 doing 7 's been 8 's been 9 's been ringing 10 've written 11 've interviewed 12 've interviewed 13 've sent 14 have/'ve phoned 15 've been looking 16 've already read 17 've read

17 1 the police arrived … the car had gone 2 I got to the shop … it had closed 3 They had eaten … I arrived 4 we left the beach … the rain had already started 5 I tried … she had left 6 I found … someone had taken 7 The car had gone … I looked 8 The patient had already died … I saw her. 9 the garages had closed … we crossed 10 Had you already left … the trouble started 11 had not arrived … left 12 got … had closed

18 By 1999, Mr and Mrs Charlton had been living in 17 Portland Street for five years. They had tried to move several times, but this had not been possible, as they were unable to sell their house. Several people had looked at the property, but (had) quickly lost interest – and the reason for this was obvious. For three years the garden of 17 Portland Street had been covered by three feet of water. The Charltons had tried to find the reason for this strange occurrence, but no one had been able to help. The water level had been rising since 1987, and had damaged the whole of the ground floor. The Charltons had been keeping the water back with sandbags, but of course this was only a temporary defence. Mrs Charlton said she had contacted the water authorities, the town council, even her local MP, but no one had been able to explain why their back garden had become a swimming pool for all the children in the neighbourhood.

19 1 left 2 was trying 3 has he called 4 've known 5 're watching 6 had already told 7 have they been 8 've been working 9 've ever met 10 noticed 11 had locked 12 don't think 13 was doing 14 had been waiting 15 jumped … ran 16 's talking 17 've had 18 've been doing 19 had been travelling 20 's having 21 don't understand 22 stayed 23 Have you been 24 had told 25 went 26 stopped 27 was using 28 have you seen 29 were arguing 30 've never trusted 31 haven't they arrived 32 've been trying 33 'd already done it 34 've ever driven 35 was making 36 had put 37 Do you agree 38 were filming 39 had been using 40 left 41 are trying 42 you've bought 43 's been working 44 had been sitting 45 's cleaning 46 hate 47 lay 48 've seen 49 had hidden 50 stayed … worked

20 1 'll go 2 're going to have 3 'm meeting 4 will be/is going to be 5 'll have to 6 are coming 7 's going to hit 8 won't do 9 is going to open 10 'll make 11 'll go 12 Are you staying/Are you going to stay. 13 is going to look for 14 's going to cry

15 'll try 16 will you do 17 's coming round/'s going to come round 18 won't do 19 's going to be 20 'll come back

21 1P 2F 3F 4P 5F 6P 7P 8F 9P 10F

22 1 'll be seeing … 'll tell 2 Will you be working 3 'll be staying 4 'll be visiting … 'll ask 5 'll be seeing … 'll give 6 won't be able … 'll be using it 7 'll be living 8 'll be sitting 9 will be staying 10 'll be flying 11 will you be doing 12 'll be coming round … 'll show 13 'll be arriving 14 won't hear/won't be hearing … 'll be 15 'll be having

23 1 won't have eaten 2 'll have been working 3 'll have met 4 'll have been studying 5 'll have lived/been living 6 'll have been working 7 'll have been standing 8 will have become 9 'll have been 10 'll have been playing 11 'll have been driving 12 won't have eaten 13 will have questioned 14 'll have been

24 1 I'll have been 2 does the train leave 3 'll be lying 4 'll be waiting … 5 'll have finished/'ll be finishing 6 Are you going to see/Will you see/Will you be seeing … 7 'll have been driving/'ll have driven 8 is starting/is going to start/ will be starting 9 will have interviewed 10 'll be living

25 1 I was going to go to university, but I failed my exams, so I left school at sixteen.
2 I was going to find a job in Madrid, but there were no jobs, so I decided to go to England to study English.
3 I was going to study English in London, but I didn't like London, so I went to Cambridge instead.
4 I was going to stay with an English family, but I changed my mind and stayed in a student hostel.
5 I was going to study English for two years, but I didn't have enough money, so I finished after eighteen months.
6 I was going to work in England when I finished school, but I couldn't find a job, so I came back to Madrid.
7 I wasn't going to work in my parents' restaurant, but I needed the money, so I did.

26

	Positive	Question	Negative
1	She agrees.	Does she agree?	She doesn't agree.
2	He's leaving.	Is he leaving?	He isn't leaving.
3	They left.	Did they leave?	They didn't leave.
4	He was shouting.	Was he shouting?	He wasn't shouting.
5	They've arrived.	Have they arrived?	They haven't arrived.
6	She's been working.	Has she been working?	She hasn't been working.
7	They'd gone.	Had they gone?	They hadn't gone.
8	They'd been sleeping.	Had they been sleeping?	They hadn't been sleeping.
9	He'll leave.	Will he leave?	He won't leave.
10	They'll be working tomorrow.	Will they be working tomorrow?	They won't be working tomorrow.
11	They'll have left by tomorrow.	Will they have left by tomorrow?	They won't have left by tomorrow.
12	They'll have been working all day.	Will they have been working all day?	They won't have been working all day.

27 1 's playing 2 went 3 'll see 4 rang … was watching … didn't answer 5 's working 6 'll live/'ll be living 7 don't like 8 didn't understand … meant … explained 9 'll make 10 rolled … smashed … hit 11 called … were all working … didn't stay 12 'll be seeing … I'll give 13 don't understand … he says/he's saying 14 are waiting 15 was rolling … caught … went

28 1 Have you seen 2 've been writing 3 haven't played 4 have you been waiting 5 had been talking 6 'll have worked/'ll have been working 7 had finished 8 'll have done 9 've been reading … haven't finished 10 had been waiting 11 've known 12 've been trying 13 will have been working 14 'd been working 15 'll have got 16 Had anyone arrived 17 's been doing 18 haven't seen 19 Have you said 20 hadn't been expecting

29a

Infinitive	Past Simple	Past Participle
bet	bet	bet
bite	bit	bitten
bleed	bled	bled
creep	crept	crept
dig	dug	dug
feed	fed	fed
flee	fled	fled
freeze	froze	frozen
hang	hung/hanged	hung/hanged
lay	laid	laid
lead	led	led
leap	leapt	leapt
mistake	mistook	mistaken
ring	rang	rung
rise	rose	risen
sew	sewed	sewn/sewed
shake	shook	shaken
shrink	shrank	shrunk
sink	sank	sunk
slide	slid	slid
spit	spat	spat
split	split	split
spread	spread	spread
stick	stuck	stuck
swing	swung	swung
tear	tore	torn
wake	woke	woken
weep	wept	wept

29b 1 has bitten 2 split 3 have dug 4 has risen 5 fled 6 Have they rung 7 Have you just woken 8 sank 9 has shrunk 10 led

30a 1 They accused me of taking the money. 2 She advised me to wait; She advised waiting for a while; She advised that they should wait. 3 We agreed to leave early; We agreed about leaving early; We agreed that we should leave early. 4 I apologized for being late. 5 Peter asked to speak to Janice; Peter asked if he could speak to Janice. 6 We began to read the instructions; We began reading the instructions. 7 We believed in telling the truth; We believed that we should tell the truth. 8 They complained about being hungry; They complained that they were hungry. 9 Mary continued to work at home; Mary continued working at home.

10 We all decided to have a picnic; We all decided that we should have a picnic; We all decided on having a picnic. 11 I dreamt/dreamed that I was flying to the moon; I dreamt/dreamed about flying to the moon. 12 They encouraged me to practise every day. 13 He enjoyed swimming a lot. 14 She expected to go to Paris for the summer; She expected that she would go to Paris for the summer. 15 They finished eating at ten. 16 I forgot to phone my mother; I forgot about phoning my mother; I forgot that I had said that I would/was going to phone my mother. 17 She hated being bored; She hated to be bored.

30b 1 A 2 A/C 3 B/C 4 A/B 5 A 6 A/B/C 7 A/B/C 8 A 9 A/B 10 A 11 A 12 B/C 13 B 14 A 15 A/C 16 A/B/C 17 A/B/C 18 A/C 19 A/B/C 20 A 21 A/B/C 22 A 23 A/B 24 A/B 25 B/C 26 B/C 27 A 28 A/B 29 A 30 A/B/C

30c

	Infinitive	Gerund	Indirect Speech
accuse		✓ of	
advise	✓	✓	✓
agree	✓	✓ on about	✓
apologize		✓ for	
ask	✓		✓
begin	✓	✓	
believe		✓ in	✓
complain		✓ about	✓
continue	✓	✓	
decide	✓	✓ on	✓
dream		✓ about	✓
encourage	✓		
enjoy		✓	
expect	✓		✓
finish	✓	✓	
forget	✓	✓ about	✓
hate	✓	✓	
help	✓		
hope	✓		✓
insist		✓ on	✓
intend	✓	✓	
invite	✓		
know	✓	✓ about	✓
learn	✓	✓ about	✓
let	✓		

[handwritten margin notes: "pedin" (by ask); "quejar" (by complain); "armar a la gente que haga algo" (by encourage); "esperar a que pase algo"]

151

love	✓	✓	
make	✓		
manage	✓		
mind		✓	✓
miss		✓	
offer	✓		
order	✓		✓
plan	✓	✓ on	✓
prefer	✓	✓	✓
promise	✓		✓
recommend	✓	✓	✓
refuse	✓		
remember	✓	✓	✓
seem	✓		
start	✓	✓	
stop	✓	✓	
suggest		✓	✓
think		✓ of about	✓
tell	✓		
try	✓	✓	
want	✓		
warn	✓	✓ against about	✓

31 1 The garages are cleaned every day. 2 He has been given a lot of money. 3 Two hundred people were arrested. 4 Every car engine is checked thoroughly. 5 This computer is exported to seventy different countries. 6 The meeting has been cancelled. 7 The factory was opened at nine o'clock. 8 Two million books are sent to America every year. 9 All the students in the school have been invited. 10 He has been told not to be late again. 11 All the letters were posted yesterday. 12 The bread is wrapped automatically. 13 I was paid a lot of money to do the job. 14 Fortunately, the machinery wasn't damaged. 15 The newspapers are sent to Scotland by train.

32a Acid rain <u>is caused</u> by burning coal or oil. When either fuel <u>is burned</u>, it releases poisonous gases which <u>are carried</u> up into the atmosphere and sometimes transported long distances.
Over 3,000 research projects <u>have been carried out</u> to look into acid rain, and a decision to tackle the problem <u>has been</u> <u>taken</u> in most of the western European countries. Measures <u>have been taken</u> in Scandinavia and in Central Europe to stop the pollution before it <u>is dumped</u> on the environment: and a diplomatic campaign <u>has been launched</u> to convince other countries that the problem has <u>to be considered</u> as a major ecological threat. 'Five years ago this issue <u>was not being taken</u> seriously.' says one leading environmental group, 'but now that damage <u>has been reported</u> in large areas of forest and lakeland, our politicians <u>are being forced</u> to take action. This problem must <u>be solved</u> quickly: if governments do nothing, they <u>will be faced</u> in two or three years' time with the accusation that they have allowed our forests to die.' A major international initiative to combat acid rain <u>is expected</u> in the near future.

32b 1 Dr Johnson's being interviewed at the moment. 2 This machine mustn't be used after 5.30p.m. 3 He had been warned the day before not to go too near the canal. 4 The outside of the ship was being painted when the accident happened. 5 This machine must be cleaned every time it is used. 6 The flowers should be kept in a warm sunny place. 7 Your shoes are being mended at the moment. 8 Your car will be driven to Edinburgh on Tuesday. 9 Smoking is not allowed in this restaurant. 10 Your bill should be paid before you leave the hotel. 11 The children have been told about the party. 12 This programme is being watched by about thirty million people. 13 Students are expected not to talk during the examination. 14 This button must not be touched while the experiment is in progress. 15 A whistle will be blown if there is an emergency. 16 The bomb was being carried to a safe place when it exploded. 17 My chair has been moved! 18 Mr and Mrs Davidson are being questioned by the police. 19 The water level is checked every week. 20 Two hundred people were invited to the wedding.

33 1 We have the newspapers delivered. 2 I had the carpets cleaned every year. 3 They're going to have their house painted. 4 We have the accounts checked every month. 5 I have the money sent to my bank account in London. 6 I'm going to have my stereo cleaned. 7 I'm having my camera repaired at the moment. 8 He spilt coffee on my jacket so he had it cleaned. 9 It's time to have the car serviced. 10 I think I'll have the office curtains changed. 11 I think I'll have the typewriter repaired. 12 We couldn't go to Jack's flat: he was having it painted. 13 We're having the computer changed. 14 I have the films processed in England. 15 I didn't want to eat in the hotel dining-room, so I had a meal sent up to my room.

34a 1 I wish I lived in Australia. 2 I wish I didn't have to go to school on Saturdays. 3 I wish we went away more often. 4 I wish I was/were a film star. 5 I wish we had a bigger house. 6 I wish I spoke more languages. 7 I wish I was/were able to/could cook. 8 I wish the school wasn't/weren't so expensive. 9 I wish I had more money. 10 I wish I didn't have to do homework every night.

34b 1 I wish I hadn't decided to work in London. 2 I wish we'd gone to Alan's party. 3 I wish we hadn't gone to live with my parents in Surrey. 4 I wish I hadn't decided to stop working as a bus driver. 5 I wish we hadn't put our money into a grocery shop. 6 I wish we hadn't borrowed £3,000 to start the business. 7 I wish we had realized that a supermarket was opening nearby. 8 I wish the grocery shop hadn't closed down. 9 I wish we hadn't lost all our money. 10 I wish we hadn't left Manchester.

34c 1 I wish John would come home before twelve o'clock. 2 I wish Sheila would be more polite to her grandparents. 3 I wish Peter would wash more often. 4 I wish Susan would work harder for her exams. 5 I wish John would help with the housework. 6 I wish Peter would give up smoking. 7 I wish Sheila wouldn't take so many days off work. 8 I wish John wouldn't play football all the time. 9 I wish Sheila and Susan wouldn't be so unkind to Peter. 10 I wish John would wear a tie more often.

35a 1 a) No b) the present 2 a) No b) the past (it's a wish in the present to change an event in the past) 3 a) No b) the present/future 4 a) Yes b) the past 5 a) No b) No c) the present 6 a) Yes b) No c) the present/future 7 a) No b) No c) the present 8 a) No b) the past

35b 1 would stop 2 hadn't snowed 3 I knew 4 wouldn't be 5 they'd visited 6 I spoke 7 hadn't been 8 I'd refused 9 I had 10 would

36 1 'll call 2 'd drive 3 lost 4 rains 5 could 6 is 7 would worry 8 'll come 9 hurry 10 would do 11 asked 12 complains 13 'd tell 14 'll meet 15 have 16 am/'m 17 spoke 18 won 19 closed 20 comes

37 1 What would you have done if I hadn't lent you the money? 2 If you had asked me for tickets, I could have got you some. 3 I wouldn't have married him if I had known what he was like. 4 I wouldn't have hired a car if I had known how expensive it was. 5 If we had got to the cinema earlier, we wouldn't have missed the start of the film. 6 If I had been born a year earlier, I wouldn't have had to do military service. 7 If you had asked me, I would have lent you my car. 8 If I had gone to university, I would have got a better job. 9 I wouldn't have gone out yesterday if you had asked me not to. 10 I could have given you a lift if my car hadn't broken down. 11 I wouldn't have gone to Berlin if I had known what was going to happen. 12 I would have stayed longer if she had wanted me to. 13 I wouldn't have come to this school if I had known what it was like. 14 We would have gone to his party if we had been able to find a baby-sitter. 15 I would have visited you in hospital if I had known you were there.

38 1 provided that 2 Just suppose 3 Imagine 4 as long as 5 unless 6 Imagine 7 So long as 8 provided that 9 unless 10 Suppose

39 1

MR A:	I don't think he should go.
MRS A:	Why not? He's sixteen, he's old enough. I'm sure <u>he wouldn't do anything stupid.</u>
MR A:	You know him – <u>he'd get involved in a fight.</u> I don't think <u>he could look after himself. He'd get hurt.</u>
MRS A:	I'm sure <u>he'd keep out of trouble.</u>
MR A:	Are you? Well I'm not. I don't think we should let him go.

2

MARTHA:	I think we should go to Scotland for the holiday. I'm fed up with going abroad and getting sick. <u>We'd enjoy ourselves more in Scotland.</u>
JAMES:	Oh, I don't think so. The weather's terrible up there. <u>We wouldn't be able to sunbathe or go swimming.</u> <u>There'd be nothing to do.</u>
MARTHA:	<u>We could go walking in the mountains.</u> <u>That would be lovely.</u>
JAMES:	Well I think <u>it would be dangerous.</u> You know what terrible mists they have in Scotland. There are always stories about people getting lost in the mountains.
MARTHA:	How about going with a group – the Youth Club, for instance?
JAMES:	Oh, you know <u>you'd hate that.</u> You can't stand organized holidays.

40 1 E 2 H 3 B 4 F 5 J 6 A 7 G 8 I 9 D 10 C

41 1 wouldn't have been 2 resigned 3 would have liked. 4 asks 5 had written 6 would he stay 7 'll ask 8 'll look after 9 had been 10 would have loved 11 see 12 don't stop 13 get 14 Will you let me know 15 was 16 will be 17 've finished 18 would be 19 see 20 look after 21 looked after 22 had looked after 23 would've enjoyed 24 wouldn't have left 25 Ask 26 wouldn't have gone out 27 would you say 28 'll be tired 29 is 30 turn

42 1 mustn't 2 Can 3 should 4 needn't 5 might 6 Could 7 ought to 8 will 9 Shall 10 may

43 1 'll be able to/can 2 couldn't/wasn't able to 3 Can/Could 4 can/'m able to 5 Can/ Could 6 Will she be able to/Can she 7 couldn't/wasn't able to 8 couldn't/ wasn't able to 9 can't/won't be able to 10 Were you able to 11 hasn't been able to 12 was able to 13 can/'ll be able to 14 couldn't/ weren't able to 15 could/ were able to

44 1 and 7; 2 and 10; 3 and 12; 4 and 11; 5 and 15; 6 and 14; 8 and 13; 9 and 16

45 1 had to 2 mustn't 3 don't have to 4 'll have to/must 5 Do you have to /Must you 6 'll have to/You must 7 's had to 8 have to/must 9 Did you have to 10 didn't have to 11 had to 12 had to/must 13 'll have to/must get 14 had to 15 mustn't

46 1 They should be in bed/They ought to be in bed. 2 They shouldn't smoke in here/ They oughtn't to smoke in here. 3 You should clean them more often/You ought to clean them more often. 4 He should drive more carefully/He ought to drive more carefully. 5 You shouldn't lend him any more/You oughtn't to lend him any more. 6 Should we take something to eat?/Ought we to take something to eat? 7 Should I wear a suit?/Ought I to wear a suit? 8 Should we pay him now?/Ought we to pay him now? 9 We shouldn't stay here/We oughtn't to stay here. 10 Maybe we should send them a present/Maybe we ought to send them a present.

47 1 should/ought to 2 have to 3 should/ ought to/ had to 4 'll have to/we have to 5 should/ought to 6 must 7 should 8 should/ought to/must 9 should/ought to 10 should/ought to 11 don't have to 12 shouldn't/oughtn't to 13 should/ought to/had to 14 should/ ought to 15 shouldn't/ oughtn't to/mustn't

48 1 needn't 2 Do I need to 3 needs 4 don't need to 5 Do I need to 6 needn't 7 need to 8 needn't 9 don't need to 10 needn't

49 1 Your house needs painting. 2 How many people do we need for a full team? 3 We need more time. 4 This floor needs cleaning. 5 The doctor says that I need more exercise. 6 Your tyres need changing. 7 How much food do we need for the weekend? 8 How much money do we need for the trip? 9 The dog needs feeding. 10 The baby needs washing.

50 1 didn't need to catch 2 needn't have lent 3 needn't have done 4 didn't need to take 5 needn't have bought 6 didn't need to take 7 didn't need to count 8 needn't have worked 9 needn't have got up 10 didn't need to stay

51 1 needn't have fixed 2 needs painting 3 need 4 needn't stay 5 do I need 6 needn't have taken 7 needn't have got up 8 needs cleaning 9 needed to have 10 needn't have sent 11 needs to work 12 needn't do/didn't need to do 13 didn't need to show 14 Do you need to have 15 needn't worry

52 1 You shouldn't have said that. 2 They might not have gone. 3 She couldn't have known. 4 The machine ought to have worked. 5 They can't have left. 6 We ought to have stopped them. 7 Should I have told the teacher? 8 Could they have helped me? 9 Ought I to have stayed? 10 He can't have been there. 11 They might not have liked it. 12 He may have agreed. 13 Shouldn't he have said something? 14 Couldn't John have driven the car? 15 Shouldn't he have checked the information?

53 1 must have told 2 could have taken 3 shouldn't have been 4 could/might have been 5 can't/couldn't have moved 6 Couldn't/Shouldn't you have been 7 can't/couldn't have known 8 should have told 9 couldn't/can't have got 10 couldn't/can't have left 11 could have gone 12 should have apologized 13 could/might have been 14 shouldn't have said 15 can't/couldn't have left 16 could/should have warned 17 must have been 18 couldn't/can't have known 19 can't/couldn't have been 20 should have let

54 1 might/could have 2 wouldn't have 3 could/would/might 4 could/might 5 would be 6 could/might 7 couldn't have 8 could/might 9 could/would/might 10 would/might 11 Would/Could 12 could/might have 13 would/could/might have 14 could/might 15 wouldn't 16 Would/Could 17 could/might 18 could have 19 might/would 20 Could

55 1 to finish 2 waiting 3 to meet 4 climbing 5 to have 6 parking 7 living 8 being 9 to lock 10 listening 11 sharing … living 12 missing 13 playing 14 to get 15 to help

56 1 your/you 2 my/me 3 our/us 4 John's/John 5 her 6 your/you 7 Mr Maslin/Mr Maslin's 8 their/them 9 their/them 10 his/him 11 their/them 12 her 13 his/him 14 our/us 15 my/me

57 1 She has a plane to catch. 2 There is a lot of housework to do. 3 Who wants something to eat? 4 He's too young to smoke. 5 I expect Jane to come. 6 I'm delighted to hear the news. 7 I have some books to read. 8 I'm surprised to hear of his illness. 9 The children have nothing to do. 10 I have some letters to write. 11 He has some shopping to do. 12 I have nothing to say. 13 You always have too much to eat. 14 It's too cold to eat outside. 15 It's lovely to see you again.

58 1 was a very strange question to ask. 2 was kind of you to visit Janice in hospital. 3 was a very rude remark to make. 4 was very exciting to fly the plane. 5 was quite a surprise to see her again. 6 was very generous of John to give them £100. 7 was very difficult to drive the car. 8 was a very odd place to visit. 9 was very silly of him to do that. 10 was stupid of him to drive/ have driven the car like that.

59 1 I saw him arrive early. 2 They made me stay at home. 3 We watched her get out of the car. 4 They let me telephone my lawyer. 5 I heard them leave at eleven o'clock. 6 The policeman made me empty my pockets. 7 I saw the dog jump through the window. 8 Do you think the school will·make me pay extra? 9 I felt the animal move. 10 Do you think the government will let me leave the country?

60 1 to have finished 2 have known 3 to have finally met 4 to have contacted 5 to have collected 6 have visited 7 to have missed 8 to have finished 9 to have been able to help 10 have told

61 1 Flying 2 to get … to eat 3 cooking 4 getting up 5 not inviting 6 to do 7 playing 8 Swimming 9 to see 10 to look after 11 to pass … copying. 12 not to phone 13 doing 14 playing 15 to go 16 not to stay 17 putting them down 18 to have 19 adding 20 seeing 21 to check 22 to go 23 not to hear 24 joining 25 to say 26 not to stay 27 being able 28 sit 29 to say 30 not to do

62 Note: *that* can be used after the main verb in all these sentences.
1 She said (that) she was very tired. 2 He said (that) he would see them soon. 3 She said (that) she was going to the cinema. 4 He said (that) he saw the children quite often. 5 She said (that) she was having a bath. 6 He said (that) he'd already met their parents. 7 She said (that) she'd stayed in a hotel for a few weeks. 8 He said (that) he had to go home to make the dinner. 9 She said (that) she hadn't been waiting long. 10 He said (that) he was listening to the radio. 11 She said (that) she'd tell them the news on Saturday. 12 He said (that) he liked swimming, dancing and playing tennis. 13 She said (that) she could drive. 14 He said (that) he'd walked home after the party. 15 She said (that) she was going to be sick. 16 He said (that) he had to go out to post a letter. 17 She said (that) she'd spoken to Jane last week. 18 He said (that) he was trying to listen to the music. 19 She said

(that) she'd phone the office from the airport. 20 He said (that) he couldn't speak any foreign languages.

63 Note: *that* can be used after the main verb in all these sentences.
1 She said (that) she'd see me the next day. 2 He said (that) he'd seen her that day. 3 She said (that) she didn't like the film. 4 She said (that) they'd gone swimming that day. 5 She said (that) she'd see Mary the following Sunday. 6 He said (that) he'd met her about three months previously/before. 7 She said (that) Pete and Sue were getting married the next day. 8 He said (that) Stephen was bringing some records to the party that night. 9 She said (that) she really liked the furniture. 10 She said (that) her parents were arriving the next day. 11 They said (that) they had visited her that morning. 12 They said (that) they'd see her the following week. 13 He said (that) they had been there three months before/previously. 14 He said (that) he was meeting them at four o'clock that day. 15 She said (that) she could see me the following day.

64 1 He wanted to know what my name was. 2 She asked how old I was. 3 I asked when the train left. 4 He asked how I was. 5 My mother wanted to know who I had seen at the meeting. 6 He wanted to know why I had taken his wallet. 7 She asked how I had got to school. 8 The boy wanted to know where I lived. 9 She asked why Judy hadn't been at the party. 10 My father wanted to know why I hadn't telephoned. 11 The teacher demanded to know why I was so late. 12 The judge inquired why the police hadn't reported the crime. 13 He demanded to know why I wouldn't let him in. 14 We inquired what time the plane arrived. 15 She asked who I wanted to talk to.

65 Note: *whether* can be used instead of *if* in all these sentences.
1 She asked if/whether I liked Marlon Brando. 2 He asked if/whether I was enjoying myself. 3 She asked if/whether my father worked there. 4 He asked if I

lived near my family. 5 She asked if I was a foreigner. 6 He asked if I had met Danny before. 7 She asked if I was hungry. 8 He asked if I had borrowed his dictionary. 9 She asked if I had finished my exams. 10 He asked if I had invited Judy and Pat. 11 She asked if my brother lived in London. 12 He asked if I knew who had broken the window. 13 She asked if they had told me when they were leaving. 14 He asked if I had lent them my camera. 15 She asked if I had hurt myself.

66 1 He wanted to know which book I had taken. 2 She wanted to know if/whether I was wearing my overcoat. 3 He wanted to know if/whether I had telephoned my mother. 4 She wanted to know if/whether the box was made of cardboard. 5 He wanted to know how much it had cost. 6 She wanted to know if/whether I was seeing the director the next day. 7 He wanted to know what I was doing. 8 She wanted to know how far she had to walk. 9 He wanted to know if/whether I had had anything to eat. 10 She wanted to know if/whether I was in a hurry. 11 He wanted to know when the performance started. 12 She wanted to know how long the journey took. 13 He wanted to know where I had stayed in Paris. 14 She wanted to know if/whether I had had any letters. 15 He wanted to know if/whether I liked having holidays abroad. 16 She wanted to know if/whether I had seen the accident. 17 He wanted to know which school I had gone to. 18 She wanted to know when I had started learning Spanish. 19 He wanted to know if/whether I was French. 20 She wanted to know if/whether I had ever been to Japan.

67 1 He told Mary to sit down. 2 The children's mother warned them not to go near the sea. 3 Tim's father told him not to be late. 4 The librarian told the children to be quiet. 5 The officer ordered the men not to shoot. 6 The inspector told us to have our tickets ready. 7 The landlady told us not to use the telephone after eleven o'clock. 8 The receptionist told us to leave our keys on the desk. 9 The customs officer told us to have our passports ready. 10 My boss told me to finish the job tonight/that night. 11 The general ordered the soldiers to run. 12 My mother told me to open the door. 13 My father told me not to spend too much money on my holiday. 14 He told me to hurry up. 15 She told me not to be frightened.

68 1 He asked me to pass his suitcase. 2 She asked if I would like some coffee. 3 He asked me to take the children to school for him. 4 She asked me to sit down. 5 He asked me to talk more quietly. 6 She asked if I would like a lift into town. 7 He asked if I would like to go out at the weekend. 8 She asked me to turn on the radio. 9 He asked me to move my car. 10 She asked if I would like to eat in the hotel or in a restaurant. 11 He asked me to pass his cup. 12 She asked me to check the oil. 13 He asked me to turn the car engine off. 14 She asked if I would like to stay with them. 15 He asked me to check the bill for him.

69 1 had … spoken 2 to take off 3 had been living 4 not to go 5 had … left 6 to check 7 hadn't eaten 8 would see 9 would like 10 to give 11 to stay back 12 will be coming back/is coming back 13 I was 14 had to be switched off 15 to open 16 had registered 17 to stay 18 are having 19 was leaving 20 had 21 decided 22 not to smoke 23 are not going to accept 24 didn't know 25 had not been 26 agreed 27 couldn't … were going to go 28 not too say … to listen 29 had arrived … had come 30 had talked

70 1 She announced that they were going to get married in June. 2 She warned him not to go near the dog. 3 After the meal, he insisted on paying. 4 She apologized for not writing. 5 He invited them to come/go round for dinner on Friday evening. 6 The doctor advised her to give up smoking. 7 He admitted that he had been wrong and I had been right. 8 She promised to write every week. 9 She offered to carry the suitcase for me.

10 He suggested going to the theatre on Saturday. 11 The Prime Minister claimed that the newspaper report wasn't true. 12 She reminded him to post the letter. 13 The teacher agreed that it was a difficult exam. 14 The manager refused to give her a pay rise. 15 She boasted that her parents had three cars.

71 There are several ways of summarizing this conversation, so there is not a 'right' answer. This is a suggested summary: 'Oh, I saw David today. He suggested taking Mum and Dad to a restaurant called "Le Pain". He also said we could leave the kids with him and Jackie on Saturday night. Jackie got that job with the BBC. Isn't that marvellous? Anyway, I invited them round for lunch on Sunday…'

72 1 I have paid him all the money. 2 He brought me a lovely bunch of flowers. 3 I hope you have bought a present for your grandmother. 4 Can you give me the money for some new shoes? 5 I'd like you to take this fruit to your mother. 6 I am hoping they will give me a new job. 7 Please can you find the train timetable for Rose? 8 I gave your letter to Andrew. 9 Why don't you show her the garden? 10 I will make a drink for everybody.

73 1 We had a good time at the party yesterday. 2 She played very well at the stadium last week. 3 The children played quietly in the garden this afternoon. 4 He drove very quickly through the town. 5 He sat quietly in his chair all through the afternoon. 6 They waited patiently in the rain for two or three hours. 7 The plane flew slowly around Heathrow Airport for about thirty minutes. 8 We searched the field thoroughly for several hours. 9 We worked hard in the studio on Sunday. 10 I walked slowly to the end of the road after getting the news. 11 He was sitting painfully on the edge of the bed when I saw him. 12 They were arguing furiously in the kitchen when I left. 13 The dog climbed slowly up the stairs. 14 He talked loudly and confidently for several hours. 15 She was walking slowly round the hospital ward when I saw her.

74 1 They never got 2 I've sometimes seen them/I've seen them sometimes 3 I occasionally talked to them./I talked to them occasionally. 4 I occasionally phoned him/I phoned him occasionally 5 We'll never see them again. 6 I had frequently written to them/I had written to them frequently 7 Do you often watch this programme?/Do you watch this programme often? 8 I've never been 9 She often asked how you were. 10 I've frequently complained/I've complained frequently 11 Don't you ever hear 12 I'll always remember 13 I've occasionally seen him/I've seen him occasionally in the supermarket./I've seen him in the supermarket occasionally. 14 we would never meet again 15 I've hardly ever spoken 16 We seldom saw them 17 We've always sent 18 Those children are always playing 19 They've often been waiting 20 He's always been working

75 1 We bought some lovely old German glasses. 2 Have you seen his nice new Italian sports car? 3 He lived in a dirty old wooden hut. 4 She was wearing a beautiful black and white silk shirt. 5 It's just another strange old country custom. 6 We stood under an enormous old wooden statue. 7 They gave him a beautiful silver clock. 8 I bought a large red and white striped tablecloth. 9 It was a lovely old green woollen scarf. 10 They sent him some very expensive blue and white china plates.

76 1 Although he seemed a friendly person, I didn't like him. 2 My car wouldn't start, whereas Jenny's started immediately. 3 Jo never helped with the housework, whereas Pat did. 4 In spite of living in Germany for ten years, he never learned German. 5 We sometimes stayed out late, though we always got home before twelve. 6 He didn't like sport: however, he didn't mind watching the football. 7 In spite of having eaten an hour earlier, I was very hungry. 8 Although the flat was expensive, it was very ecomfortable. 9 My parents were angry, though they soon forgave me. 10 The old house was near the sea, whereas the new one is in the middle of town.

77 1 were you talking to? 2 was talking to you? 3 telephoned me? 4 did they want to see? 5 sold the car? 6 gave you this money? 7 did you tell about the contract? 8 have they invited to the party? 9 were they arguing with? 10 complained to the manager? 11 wrote a letter the school? 12 didn't you like? 13 opened the window? 14 did she ask to help? 15 wasn't at the meeting?

78 1 It's cold isn't it? 2 He isn't very friendly, is he? 3 You don't like eggs, do you? 4 I'm staying too, aren't I? 5 They're policemen, aren't they? 6 She didn't arrive yesterday, did she? 7 This shop's very expensive, isn't it? 8 She's gone home, hasn't she? 9 This water's hot, isn't it? 10 They're not coming this afternoon, are they? 11 You haven't met my sister Jean, have you? 12 He wasn't waiting at home for me, was he? 13 She didn't like Pat when she met her, did she? 14 They're going to write to us after they move, aren't they? 15 He's got no money at the moment, has he? 16 You liked some of the music you heard today, didn't you? 17 You've nearly finished your book, haven't you? 18 You're always forgetting your keys, aren't you? 19 They've nearly finished the new school, haven't they? 20 She's not very happy in her new job, is she?

79 1 'No, I'm not.' 2 'Yes, they are.' 3 'Yes, I did.' 4 'No, she hasn't.' 5 'No, they didn't.' 6 'No, I haven't.' 7 'Yes, she has.' 8 'No, she isn't.' 9 'Yes, I have.' 10 'No, he isn't.'

80 1 'No, I won't.' 2 'Yes, they did.' 3 'Yes, I have.' 4 'Yes, there is.' 5 'Yes, I have.' 6 'No, I haven't.' 7 'No, they weren't.' 8 'No, they aren't.' 9 'Yes, he is.' 10 'No, I won't.' 11 'No, they haven't.' 12 'No, he isn't.' 13 'No, they haven't.' 14 'No, she hadn't.' 15 'Yes, it is.' 16 'No, I don't.' 17 'Yes, he did.' 18 'No, I won't.' 19 'Yes, it is.' 20 'No, you didn't.'

81 1 Could you tell me when the train leaves? 2 Do you think that it's going to rain today? 3 Do you know if everybody has left already? 4 Do you think you could tell me what time it is, please? 5 Do you know why there is nobody here? 6 Could you tell me why you left so early? 7 Do you know if the meeting is cancelled? 8 Do you think there will be a lot of people at the party? 9 Could you tell me what time this shop closes? 10 Do you know how much this is? 11 Do you think you could tell me when the plane from Paris arrives? 12 Do you think there will be another train tonight? 13 Could you tell me when you will be finished? 14 Do you know how long we will have to wait? 15 Do you think you could tell me where the post office is?

82 1 Yes, I think so. 2 No, I don't suppose so. 3 Yes, I expect so. 4 No, I don't suppose so. 5 No, I hope not. 6 No, I don't think so. 7 No, I hope not. 8 Yes, I expect so. 9 Yes, I think so. 10 Yes, I suppose so.

83 1 The woman who I spoke to wasn't very polite. (O) 2 The machine that worked better than the others cost the least.(S) 3 I wouldn't stay in a hotel that refused to accept children. (S) 4 I don't understand people who hate animals. (S) 5 The stereo that I bought last week doesn't work properly. (O) 6 The television that they have designed is going to be very expensive. (O) 7 That man who complained is always making trouble. (S) 8 The woman who gave us all this money is not very rich. (S) 9 I admire people who can speak more than one language. (S) 10 The assistant who you complained about has been moved. (O)

84 1 The man I shouted at didn't come back again. 2 The television I dropped never worked again. 3 The machine I hired was broken. 4 The clothes she bought were beautiful. 5 The wall they built fell down after three weeks. 6 The policeman I asked wasn't very helpful. 7 I didn't really like the car we bought. 8 I lost the money I borrowed from Janice. 9 I really liked the new teacher they sent. 10 I had a terrible argument with the sales assistant I sacked.

85 1 There's the lady whose dog was killed. 2 That's the man who's going to buy the company. 3 He's the person whose car was stolen. 4 She's the new doctor who's coming to the hospital next month. 5 She's the journalist whose article was on the front page of *The Times*. 6 They're the people whose shop burned down last week. 7 That's the sales director who's leaving in March. 8 That's the student whose parents complained about the school. 9 She's the singer who's just signed a contract with a recording company. 10 He's the person who's going to be promoted. 11 I'm the one whose flat was broken into. 12 She's the person who's working for the film studios. 13 That's the architect who's just won a prize for design. 14 That's the boy who's just got a place at university 15 I'm the person whose flat you stayed in.

86 1 ND 2 D 3 D 4 ND 5 D 6 ND 7 ND 8 ND 9 D 10 D

87 1 – 2 who 3 that 4 who 5 – 6 which 7 who 8 who 9 which 10 – 11 who 12 who 13 which 14 – 15 –

88 1 I love the countryside, which is why I want to go and live there. 2 They stayed for hours, which I was very annoyed about. 3 He passed all his exams, which surprised us. 4 They forgot about my birthday, which was a bit disappointing. 5 The pilot showed us how to fly the plane, which was extremely interesting. 6 I couldn't get a flight to Malaga, which upset the children. 7 He was rude and aggressive, which made me very angry. 8 They said they couldn't pay for the car immediately, which made me a bit suspicious. 9 The policeman asked me for directions, which confused me a little. 10 The restaurant wouldn't accept cheques, which I found rather surprising.

89 1 where 2 when 3 where 4 where 5 when 6 why 7 where 8 when 9 where 10 why 11 when 12 when 13 where 14 when 15 when

90 1 off 2 round 3 at 4 over 5 on 6 in 7 down 8 out of 9 through 10 under

91 1 above 2 behind 3 against 4 below 5 between 6 past 7 above 8 behind 9 in front of 10 below 11 against 12 on top of

92 1 grown up 2 look after 3 've run out of 4 broke down 5 wake up 6 found out 7 looked up 8 stand up 9 kept on 10 put off 11 set off 12 told off 13 gave up 14 getting over/got over 15 going on 16 Look out 17 turned down 18 've been sitting down 19 let down 20 blew up

93 1 passed away 2 to sleep in 3 get by 4 set off 5 had grown up/grew up 6 take off?

94 1 How do you slow down the machine?/ How do you slow the machine down? 2 The company decided to give away a hundred pounds./The company decided to give a hundred pounds away. 3 I turned the television on./I turned on the television. 4 would you like to try it on? 5 The government wants to close down the factory./The government want to close the factory down. 6 I think we'll have to call it off. 7 I couldn't accept his offer so I turned him down. 8 would you pick her up?

95 1 don't you think she takes after her? 2 He never got over her death. 3 She lives off that. 4 I looked after the children. 5 you'll have to do without them. 6 He asked after you.

96 1 run out of 2 looks down on 3 goes back on 4 kept on at 5 came up with

98b 1 getting at 2 put up with 3 gone off 4 turning up 5 drifting in 6 got hold of 7 picking on 8 stormed out 9 handed in 10 picked up 11 took up 12 came up with 13 worked out

TEST 1
Part A
1 dogs' heads
2 children's
3 girls' jackets
4 laboratory door
5 the front of the house
6 week's holiday
7 kitchen door

8   doctor's receptionist
9   manager of the London office
10   six day's work.

Part B
1   –
2   an
3   –
4   the
5   a
6   the
7   a
8   –
9   The
10   the

Part C
1   the highest
2   taller than
3   the most expensive
4   the most intelligent
5   shorter than
6   the ugliest
7   the most wonderful
8   the laziest
9   more expensive
10   better than

Part D
1   Were you frightened of the wolves?
2   The ladies walked quickly out of the room.
3   The room was full of shelves.
4   There were a lot of people at the party.
5   They packed everything into boxes.
6   Could I have a tin of peas, please?
7   A lot of people wear fur now.
8   The machine's made of silver.
9   It was a terrible experience.
10   She's a sculptor – she works with stone.

Part E
1   such
2   so
3   so
4   so
5   such
6   so
7   such
8   such
9   so
10   such

TEST 2
Part A
(1) 'm staying (2) 're looking at (3) know
(4) 're having (5) Are you enjoying (6) believe
(7) 're visiting (8) start (9) finish (10) 'm
studying (11) know (12) 'm writing (13) is
working (14) lives (15) 's sitting

Part B
1   I've broken
2   I've lived
3   We moved
4   Have you been
5   I've been
6   shouted
7   I've never done
8   He said
9   apologized
10   stayed
11   She's had
12   looked
13   did she die?
14   He's just left.
15   I've worked

Part C
1   Shall I carry your suitcase for you?
2   Wait a minute – I'll open the door.
3   The plane to Paris leaves at ten, stops at Amsterdam and arrives at twelve.
4   Look at those clouds. It's going to rain.
5   I'll never speak to him again.
6   Will she study history at university?
7   Next November we'll have been married for fifteen years.
8   I was going to leave early because it was raining, but I didn't.
9   My mother will be angry when she finds out.
10   He'll hate me if he can't come to the party.

Part D
1   The aeroplanes are checked every month.
2   He has been given some new clothes.
3   The rooms are cleaned every evening.
4   Two million copies of the books were sold last year.
5   The examination papers are checked in this room.
6   As soon as you arrive in the hospital, your temperature is checked.

7   He hasn't been invited.
8   The lorries are sent by aeroplane.
9   The gates are opened at ten o'clock.
10   This film was directed by Steven Spielberg.

TEST 3
Part A
1   wouldn't have been
2   invite
3   'll make
4   would have enjoyed
5   happens
6   would have had
7   answer
8   'll be
9   stops
10   were

Part B
1   Could
2   needn't
3   should
4   might
5   Can
6   couldn't
7   can't
8   don't have to
9   mustn't
10   didn't have to

Part C
1   can't have taken
2   could have left
3   should have phoned
4   could have driven
5   should have been
6   must have heard
7   should have stopped
8   shouldn't have gone out
9   must have taken
10   could have gone

Part D
1   He asked me which coat I had taken.
2   He said he would see me on the following
     Tuesday.
3   They asked me how much it was.
4   She asked me to hurry up.
5   He asked me to sit down.
6   She said she couldn't do it.
7   She said she'd send an e-mail from the

airport.
8   He asked me to turn on the computer.
9   He asked why he couldn't connect to the
     Internet.
10   He said he was sorry he was late.

Part E
1   No, she won't.
2   Yes, I did.
3   No, they aren't.
4   No, I haven't.
5   Yes, they have.
6   No, I don't.
7   Yes, we have.
8   No, they wouldn't.
9   No, it doesn't.
10   Yes, she will.

Index

Note that all numbers in this index are page numbers.

A

a	1-4
able to, be	64
active and passive	43
adjectives	
comparative	8-9
superlative	8-9
+ infinitive	80
order of	109
possessive	4, 79
adverbial phrases	105
adverbs	
frequency	107
order of	105
although	110
article	
definite	1-2, 4
indefinite	1-2, 4
aspects	
simple and continuous	34-35
perfect	36
at	128

B

be able to	64

C

can	63-64, 76
can't have	73-74
clauses,	
contact	120
defining/non-defining	123-124
relative	119-120, 123-126
followed by which	125
commands, reported	95
comparative adjectives	8-9
conditional, the	54
first conditional	54
second conditional	54
third conditional	56
hidden conditions	59
mixed tense conditional	60
zero conditional	54
conjunctions – see link words	
contact clauses	120
continuous aspect	34-35
could	63-64
could have	73-74
countable nouns	1

/

D

'd	20-21, 51, 55
defining relative clauses	119-120, 123-126
definite article	1-2, 4

E

embedded questions	116-117
expect so/not	118

F

first conditional	54
for + *future perfect*	30
frequency adverbs	107
future, the	25-33
present continuous as future	25
going to	25
future simple	25
present simple as future	26-27
future continuous	28
future perfect	30
future in the past	33

G

gerund, the	38, 78-79
possessive + gerund	79
verbs + gerund	78
going to	25
going to, was	33

H

had to	66
have got to	65
have something done	47-48
have to	65-68
hidden conditions	59
hope so/not	118
how	105
however	110

I

if	54, 56, 56-60
indefinite article	1-2, 4
indirect speech	38, 87, 89-90, 92-93, 95, 97, 100, 102
infinitive, the	38, 78, 80-84
after certain verbs	78
after it	81
after nouns and adjectives	80
without to	82
perfect infinitive	83
in spite of	110
irregular verbs	37
it + *infinitive*	81
it's	11

L
link words   110-111

M
manner, adverbs of   105
may   63, 74, 76
may have   73-74
might   63, 74-76
might have   73-76
mixed tense conditionals   60
modals   63-77
   modals in past tense   64, 66, 71, 73-76
more ... than   8-9
most   8-9
much   9
must   63, 65-66, 68
must have   73

N
need   63, 69-71
never   107
non-defining relative clauses   123, 125-126
normally   107
nouns
   countable nouns   1
   uncountable nouns   2
   singular   6
   plural   6
   + infinitive   80

O
object, the   79, 104
occasionally   107
of (*possessive*)   4
often   107
order of adjectives   109
order of adverbs   105
ought to   67-68
ought to have   73

P
passive, the   43-45, 47-48
past continuous   15-16
past perfect   20
past perfect continuous   21
past simple   15, 18
   passive   43-45
past tenses, the   15-22
perfect aspect, the   36
perfect infinitive   83
phrasal verbs   129
plural nouns   6
possessive adjective   79

possessive of	4-5
possessive 's, s'	4-5
prepositions	128
used in idioms	128
present continuous,	11-14
as future	25
present perfect simple	17
continuous	19
passive	43-45
present simple	11-14
verbs using present simple	13
passive	43-45
present tense, the	11-14
provided that	58

Q

questions	
embedded questions	116
reported questions	90, 92, 93
tag questions	113, 114
who *questions*	111

R

rarely	107
relative clauses	119, 127
as subject or object	120
containing where, when, *or* why	126
without who *or* that	120
remember + *gerund/infinitive*	84
reported speech	87-103
commands	95
requests	97
questions	90
statements	87, 89
reporting conversations	102
requests, reported	97

S

's	4-5
s'	4-5
second conditional	54
seldom	107
shall	63, 68, 87
short answers	115
should	63, 67-68, 73-74, 87
should have	73-74
simple aspect, the	34-35
simple past – see past simple	
singular nouns	6
so	10
sometimes	107

speech, indirect or reported	87, 103
statements, reported	87, 89
stop + *gerund/infinitive*	84
subject	50-51
such	10
superlative adjectives	8, 9
suppose so/not	118

T

tag questions	113, 114
tenses, the	
present	11, 14, 22
past simple and continuous	15, 16, 22,
present perfect	17, 19, 22
past perfect	20, 21, 22
future	25, 33
tense check	34
that	
+ *infinitive*	81
+ *in relative clauses*	120-124
+ *in reported speech*	87
there ... + *infinitive*	81
think so/not	118
third conditional	56, 60
though	110
to + *infinitive*	80, 81, 83

U

uncountable nouns	2
unless	58
usually	107

V

verb, the	11, 53
irregular	37
phrasal	129, 136
taking gerund, infinitive,	
for indirect speech	38
used in reporting	100

W

what	111
what time	116
when	126
where	126
whereas	110
whether	92
which	120, 123-125
who	111, 119-120, 123-124
whose	121
why	126
wh *questions*	111
will	25, 28, 30

wish
+ *past simple*   48-49
+ *past perfect*   48, 50
+ would   48, 51
word order   104-105, 107, 109-110
would   63, 76
would have   56, 73